Recipes
from a
Deep South Inn

❖

Edna Holland

❖

Illustrations by
LOIS LEONARD STOCK

Country Roads Press
OAKS • PENNSYLVANIA

Recipes from a Deep South Inn
© 1994 by Edna Holland. All rights reserved.

Published by Country Roads Press
P.O. Box 838, 2170 West Drive
Oaks, PA 19456

Text and cover design by Amy Fischer Design.
Cover photographs by Cindy's Photography, Meridian, Mississippi.
Illustrations by Lois Stock.
Typesetting by Typeworks.

ISBN 1-56626-040-X

Printed in the United States of America.
10 9 8 7 6 5 4

Library of Congress Cataloging-in-Publication Data

Holland, Edna, 1931–
    Recipes from a deep south inn / Edna Holland.
        p.   cm.
    Includes index.
    ISBN 1-56626-040-X :
    1. Cookery, American—Southern style.   2. Hamilton Hall (Inn :
Meridian, Miss.)   I. Title.
TX715.2.S68H65   1994
641.5975—dc20
                                                    93-39791
                                                        CIP

Recipes from a Deep South Inn

For my grandmother
LILLIE CAIN MILLS
1880–1974
She taught me about cooking.
She taught me about love.

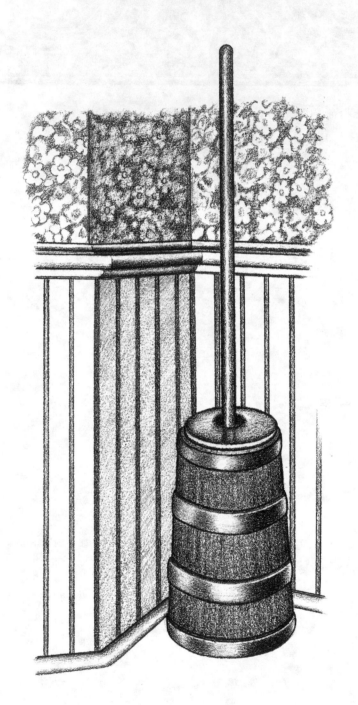

CONTENTS

PREFACE

My credentials for writing this preface are not that numerous or outstanding. I'm not a chef; however, I am a fair "everyday cook." The most logical reason I can think of is the fact that Edna has been feeding me for almost forty-four years. Food for the stomach, the soul, the mind, the heart; feeding me like no other dutiful, devoted, loving, and lovely wife could or would. How well I remember those simple dinners served to a husband by a very young bride. Each night the breaded pork chops, canned green peas, tossed salad, and lemon icebox pie tasted better than they had the night before. After a week or ten days, a new menu was introduced, and at that point in time, I knew I had a budding gourmet cook of my very own. Today Edna is recognized as one of the best cooks in the South. On the pages of *Recipes from a Deep South Inn* you'll find everything from simple southern dishes to delectable gourmet delights that any chef would be proud to serve.

It has been Edna's pleasure to serve people from around the world. Businessmen from Europe were invited to a meeting in Meridian by their company for a second time, and their company was told, "We'll return again if you will take us to Hamilton Hall for more of that wonderful food." A number of world-famous entertainers have dined with us, along with a host of educators from Asia. It is always a thrill to entertain guests from coast to coast who are in Meridian on business or pleasure. Edna has touched the lives of hundreds of newlyweds by catering their receptions, rehearsal dinners, and bridesmaids' luncheons. How often a bride has requested a recipe for a dish to serve her friends or family.

Edna has never taken a recipe and served it "as is." She must add to a recipe or take from it to give it that flare for which she is so famous. She has a wonderful staff to assist her; however, when it comes time to "cook," Edna is at the stove making sure the food is prepared just right before it goes to the table. No chef or cook for her. Every recipe in this cookbook has been tried and tasted by Edna.

Years ago, Edna started a weekly column in *Mississippi Magic*, a local newspaper. Most weeks she will tell a story relating to the recipe for the week. Through the years, her readers have told her they enjoy the stories as much as the recipes. Some of these stories are found in this cookbook.

I trust you will enjoy Edna's labor of love—her many years of preparing for this cookbook, trying many recipes that did not meet her standards and finally deciding which recipes to include, while keeping the others in the file for yet another book.

Guests come and they go at Hamilton Hall, and many return again and again. It is my hope that you will enjoy these recipes, and that you will someday visit Hamilton Hall. As for me, I'm staying! I want to break bread with my wife for another forty-four years.

—Bob Holland

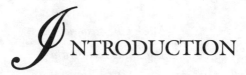

INTRODUCTION

Although Hamilton Hall was built in 1890 as a private residence, we are only the third family to occupy the house. Located in Meridian, Mississippi, it was built by a local businessman, Joe Meyer, who had many interests in this area, including being the founder of our onetime popular and beautiful Lamar Hotel, built in 1927, which was "the place for parties and dinner."

The house is a picturesque two-story Victorian boasting leaded, beveled stained-glass windows, parquet floors, and ornate hand-carved woodwork. It is one of the few houses of that era still remaining in the city. We actually purchased the house twice—the first time we saw it, with our hearts; the second time, with our money. That was in August of 1980; we moved in September and started entertaining in November. What actually started out as a hobby has turned into more than a full-time job.

Hamilton Hall would not have been possible without the help of my wonderful and devoted mother, Cornelia Ambrose. She has done just about anything I have asked of her, always with a smile and the words, "I'll try."

We have a wonderful staff, among whom are three long-time associates—Barbara Self, Jo McLellan, and Janelle Clay. They remain throughout the bad times as well as the good, undaunted by what may have happened the day before or how late they had worked the night before.

Although Hamilton Hall is an inn, it is also our home, so there is always something cooking in the kitchen, and that is reflected in the selection of recipes in this book. Since the premise of the book is to reflect the foods of the Deep South, I have included some foods that perhaps are not quite as popular in other parts of the country, and may not be considered very sophisticated. There were absolutely hundreds of recipes to choose from, and decisions did not come easily.

There are many party menus, of course, but I tried also to include some menus that contain recipes that are favorites of friends and family.

We have learned a lot since we made the decision to open Hamilton Hall. Good food is an absolute must and is expected—but there is nothing that can take the place of something the South is noted for—a friendly face and warm hospitality.

—Edna Holland

Mock Champagne

Sausage and Egg Strata

Hot Curried Fruit Towers

Garlic Cheese Grits

Ree's Biscuits

Nutty Cinnamon Coffee Cake

◆

Bloody Marys

Bacon Cheese Fingers

Crab and Shrimp Galore

Fried Grits

Fried Apple Rings with Cheese

Fresh Asparagus (see page 90)

Carrot Muffins

Strawberry or Lemon Crepes

◆

Mint Juleps

Clam Puffs

Eggs Benedict

Fresh Fruit (see page 80)

Banana Nut Bread

Cheesecake Squares

A
Mississippi
Morning
Affair

❖

We love morning affairs at Hamilton Hall and like to have menus that can be prepared in advance. You can have fun with these—just mix and match.

MOCK CHAMPAGNE

16 6-OUNCE SERVINGS

48 ounces white grape juice
48 ounces ginger ale

juice of 2 lemons

Combine the white grape juice and ginger ale in a large punch bowl. Add lemon juice. Serve well chilled.

I like to float sliced strawberries in the glasses.

This is wonderful to use when you don't know how many are coming, or for large crowds, because you can keep the ingredients on hand and mix at the last minute. Have lots. Your guests will love it.

SAUSAGE AND EGG STRATA

SERVES 10

halve —

8 slices of white bread, trimmed of the crust and cut into small cubes
½ cup butter, melted
6 eggs, well beaten
1 teaspoon dry mustard
1 tablespoon Worcestershire sauce
3 small green onions, minced

½ teaspoon salt
½ teaspoon white pepper
3 cups milk
1½ cups sharp cheddar cheese, grated
½ pound hot sausage, crumbled
½ pound mild sausage, crumbled
paprika

Butter a flat 3-quart glass baking dish. Place bread cubes on bottom of dish. Pour melted butter over cubes. Stir together the eggs, seasonings, and milk. Pour egg mixture over bread. Sprinkle with grated cheese.

Mix sausages together and brown in a skillet and drain off all the grease. I blot the sausage on paper towels. Put sausage over the cheese. Sprinkle with paprika. Cover and refrigerate 24 hours. Remove from refrigerator and bring to room temperature. Place baking dish in a slightly larger pan with ½ inch of water added. Bake uncovered at 325° for 1 hour.

This is a great morning party recipe because it has to be prepared the day before. We have made it in huge pans for as many as 300 guests for brunch wedding receptions. It has never failed us, although it does take much longer to cook when the large gas ovens are filled with pan after pan of this wonderful treat.

Hot Curried Fruit Towers

SERVES 10

1 20-ounce can Dole pineapple slices
1 29-ounce can pear halves
1 29-ounce can peach halves
1 16-ounce can apricot halves

10 maraschino cherries
⅓ cup butter
¾ cup light brown sugar
2 teaspoons curry powder

Drain fruit well and dry off large pieces with a paper towel. Lay pineapple slices down in a large, flat, glass baking dish. Top each pineapple slice with either a peach half or a pear half. On top of each of these put an apricot half. Then top with a cherry. These will resemble towers and you will need one tower for each serving. Melt the butter and add the brown sugar and curry powder. Spoon over the fruit. Bake at 325° for 1 hour, basting with the butter and sugar. Cool, refrigerate overnight, and reheat at 325° for about 30 minutes before serving.

This is another wonderful morning dish, since it is made the day before and only needs reheating. The towers are pretty whether on a buffet table on a tray or on individual serving plates. It may seem like a lot of fruit per person, but it really isn't. It also might be smart to count your fruit pieces before you begin, since sometimes a can will vary as to the number of pieces of fruit. You can wait until the day you will be serving to make this, but the fruit will not have quite as much flavor.

GARLIC CHEESE GRITS

SERVES 10

4 cups boiling water
½ teaspoon salt
1 cup grits (Quaker quick grits)
2 6-ounce rolls garlic cheese, cut into small
  pieces
½ cup butter, melted

2 eggs, well beaten
1 small clove garlic, minced
⅛ teaspoon cayenne pepper
½ cup sharp cheddar cheese, grated
paprika

Slowly pour grits into boiling salted water and cook about 5 minutes, stirring while cooking. Remove from heat and add garlic cheese and butter and stir well. Add eggs and garlic and cayenne pepper. Pour grits into flat, buttered 3-quart casserole. Sprinkle with the grated cheese and paprika. Bake at 375° for 35 to 40 minutes.

Grits are a staple here in the South. We wouldn't think of entertaining at brunch without them. We love serving them to our overnight guests, as some have never seen them before. Bob loves to tell the story of asking one gentleman if he had ever had grits before. When he replied that he hadn't, Bob insisted that he really must try some for breakfast the next morning. The gentleman replied, "Okay, I'll try just one!"

REE'S BISCUITS

SERVES 10

1½ cups Gold Medal self-rising flour,
   sifted
½ cup Crisco

1 cup buttermilk
2 pinches (scant ¼ teaspoon) baking soda

Cut shortening into flour until it resembles coarse cornmeal. Stir baking soda into the buttermilk. Add buttermilk to flour and stir quickly until mixed. Pour onto lightly floured breadboard. Roll into a ball of dough. If dough feels too soft, work a little flour in on the board. Roll out and cut with a small biscuit cutter, dipping in flour before each cut. Put the biscuits on a lightly greased baking sheet. Before baking, brush them lightly with melted butter, or margarine, or put a small amount of butter, without melting, on each biscuit. Bake in a 450° oven until brown.

This dear lady, Marie Harrington, has been making the biscuits for the Kentucky Ham Breakfast at the First Christian Church for nineteen years. This means she has to get up at 3:30 A.M. to get to the church and have the biscuits ready to start serving at 6 A.M., for three days straight. Many people flock to the church just to eat Ree's biscuits. You see, she knows just how to handle the dough and just how thin to roll it. When I asked for a secret, I was told that "the dough just has to feel comfortable."

NUTTY CINNAMON COFFEE CAKE

SERVES 10 TO 12

2¼ cups all-purpose flour
½ teaspoon salt
1 teaspoon cinnamon
¼ teaspoon ginger
1 cup brown sugar
¾ cup sugar
¾ cup Puritan oil

1 teaspoon baking soda
1 teaspoon baking powder
1 egg, beaten
1 cup buttermilk
1 cup walnuts, chopped
1 teaspoon cinnamon

Mix together the flour, salt, cinnamon, ginger, brown sugar, sugar, and oil. Take out ¼ of this mixture and to it add the baking soda, baking powder, egg, and buttermilk. Pour this batter into a buttered 9″ x 13″ x 2″ baking pan. Add the nuts and the additional teaspoon cinnamon to the remaining flour, sugar, and oil mixture. Mix well and sprinkle the nut mixture over the top of the batter. Bake at 350° for 45 minutes. This is a fun coffee cake. Everyone will rave, and it is so easy!

Fall does not come to the Deep South in September, as we continue to have high temperature readings and unyielding humidity. Such was the weather on September 15, 16, and 17, 1980, when the thermometer soared to 103°, and we made the move to Hamilton Hall. Our first night was spent sleeping on the floor in the den, as it took three days to move and the beds were not up. But what a joy it was to awaken to the puppy licking us on the face, the sunlight streaming through the stained-glass windows, and the birds chirping their hearts out outside. We knew we were home.

BLOODY MARYS

SERVES 12

46 ounces V-8 juice
4 tablespoons Worcestershire sauce
juice of 4 limes
8 dashes Tabasco

1½ teaspoons salt
1 teaspoon white pepper
2 cups vodka

Mix all ingredients except vodka. Refrigerate covered. When ready to serve, stir and add the vodka. May be made several days ahead. Garnish each glass with a celery or green onion fan.

Bloody Marys are definitely the favorite party drink for morning occasions in the South. Some like tomato juice, others V-8, but whichever they like, they want it hot and spicy.

BACON CHEESE FINGERS

SERVES 12

1 cup Swiss cheese, grated
8 slices bacon, cooked crisp and crumbled
4 tablespoons mayonnaise

1 tablespoon onion, grated
½ teaspoon celery salt
sandwich bread, crusts removed

Combine all ingredients except bread. Spread the mixture over the bread and bake at 325° for 10 minutes. I cut the bread in triangles after baking; however, you can cut it any way you like, before or after baking. This freezes very well.

Where do new recipes come from? How can you tell by reading whether a recipe is going to be good? These are questions that I am asked all the time. Of course, it really helps to have an ability for "mental tasting." After all, musicians can look at a piece of music and pretty much hear the music in their heads. It's the same way with recipes for me. I can read the list of ingredients and think of a certain flavor and how it will go with another flavor and how it will taste. Most of the time I'm right, but then there are some surprises. I think that this skill is one that is developed from doing a lot of cooking and reading a lot of cookbooks.

CRAB AND SHRIMP GALORE

SERVES 12

1 cup green pepper, finely chopped
2 cups celery, finely chopped
5 cups shrimp, cleaned and cut up if large
¼ teaspoon Tabasco
½ teaspoon black pepper
3 tablespoons onion, chopped

2 cups crabmeat
1½ tablespoons Worcestershire sauce
2 teaspoons Accent
1½ cups Hellmann's mayonnaise
1½ cups buttered cracker crumbs
¼ cup fresh parsley, chopped

Mix together the green pepper, celery, shrimp, Tabasco, black pepper, onion, Accent, crabmeat, and Worcestershire sauce. Add the mayonnaise and mix well. Place in a 3-quart buttered casserole and top with the buttered cracker crumbs, which have been mixed with the parsley. Bake at 350° for 30 to 40 minutes or until hot and bubbly. You will have happy people for brunch—this is always a hit!

Many people ask us how Hamilton Hall got its name. Two weeks after moving into the house, it was time for our vacation, so off we went with boxes still unpacked, lined up in the middle of the floor. While traveling to New England, we discussed what name we would give our new house. Hundreds of names were brought up and then we realized that it was so simple. We had always said that if we had another child, we would name it for Bob's paternal grandmother, Minda Hamilton Holland, of whom he was so fond. This house was indeed to become our third child—it takes all our time, lots of tender care, and our utmost attention!

FRIED GRITS

SERVES 12

2 cups cooked grits
salt and pepper to taste

2 eggs, beaten
bacon drippings for frying

Pack the cooked grits in a shallow baking pan to a thickness of about ½ inch. Cover with plastic wrap and chill in the refrigerator, preferably overnight. When the grits are firm, cut them into squares. Beat the eggs well. Heat the bacon drippings in a large, heavy skillet. Sprinkle the grits squares with salt and pepper and dip them into the eggs. Fry in the bacon drippings over medium heat until golden brown, turning once. Drain on paper towels and serve immediately.

We are always amazed when we can't find grits in other parts of the country. If you haven't tried them, you must. If you can't get them, write to your southern cousins to send you some or to the Old Mill in Pigeon Forge, Tennessee 37863. When we are traveling out of the South, Bob always takes his individual packets of instant grits with him, and on our last trip to Nova Scotia with a group, they stirred so much interest with people from Iowa, Wisconsin, and Minnesota that when we returned home we had to send them all some grits.

FRIED APPLE RINGS WITH CHEESE

SERVES 12—1 RING EACH

2 medium red cooking apples (like Roman
    Beauties or McIntosh)
2 tablespoons butter

2 tablespoons brown sugar
½ cup sharp cheddar cheese, grated

Core apples, but don't peel them. Slice into ¼-inch rings. Melt butter in medium skillet and sauté apples 2 minutes on each side. Add brown sugar and continue cooking the rings until sugar caramelizes.

Remove from pan and sprinkle with grated cheese.

Fried apples are good anytime of the day, but especially for brunch.

CARROT MUFFINS

SERVES 12

2 cups all-purpose flour
½ cup light brown sugar
¾ cup sugar
2 teaspoons baking soda
2 teaspoons cinnamon
½ teaspoon mace
½ teaspoon salt

½ pound carrots, peeled and grated
½ cup golden raisins
1 7-ounce can crushed pineapple
3 eggs, beaten
½ cup Puritan oil
2 teaspoons vanilla

Sift together the flour, brown sugar, sugar, baking soda, cinnamon, mace, and salt. Add the carrots and raisins and stir them around in the flour mixture to coat them. In another bowl combine the eggs, pineapple, oil, and vanilla. Pour the wet ingredients into the dry ingredients and stir well, but don't worry about lumps. Pour batter into well-greased muffin tins. Bake at 350° for 30 minutes. Serve the muffins while they are hot.

Muffins are especially useful for our overnight guests. Many times they comment on the variety we offer, and we do try to make them interesting.

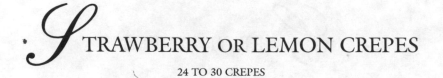

STRAWBERRY OR LEMON CREPES

24 TO 30 CREPES

CREPES

4 tablespoons butter
2 cups cake flour, sifted
½ teaspoon salt

2 cups milk
4 eggs, beaten

Melt butter and set aside. Stir together the flour and salt. Gradually add the milk, beating with a wire whisk. Add eggs and 3 tablespoons melted butter. Beat until smooth and let stand at least 30 minutes to allow flour to be absorbed. This will prevent the crepes from tearing when you turn them. Beat again before you cook the crepes.

Heat an 8- or 9-inch heavy frying pan until hot and brush lightly but thoroughly with melted butter. Pour enough crepe batter into pan to make a thin coating. Lift pan and roll mixture until bottom is covered. The amount of batter for each crepe depends on the size of the pan, so experiment until you have the correct amount. Cook about 30 seconds and loosen edges with a spatula and turn, cook another 30 seconds. When the bottom side is brown, remove to a clean dry towel.

Repeat until all batter is used. If you wish to make the crepes ahead and freeze them, wrap in clear plastic or foil, and defrost at room temperature before using.

For strawberry crepes:

FILLING

1 pint fresh strawberries, washed, hulled, and sliced
1 cup confectioners' sugar, sifted
1 8-ounce package cream cheese, softened
1 tablespoon grated lemon rind
1 tablespoon fresh lemon juice
½ teaspoon vanilla
1 cup heavy cream, whipped

SAUCE

1 pint fresh strawberries, washed, hulled, and sliced
6 tablespoons butter
⅓ cup sugar
1 tablespoon cornstarch
1 cup orange juice
½ cup Grand Marnier or orange-flavored liqueur

Combine cream cheese, confectioners' sugar, lemon juice, lemon rind, and vanilla. Fold in strawberries and whipped cream. Fill crepes with filling and roll. At serving time, warm in a 325° oven for a few minutes.

Dissolve cornstarch in orange juice. Melt 6 tablespoons butter in saucepan and add strawberries and sugar. Slowly stir in the orange juice and cornstarch mixture. Cook until slightly thickened and clear. Set aside. When ready to serve, bring sauce to a boil and stir in Grand Marnier or liqueur. Pour some of the sauce over each serving of crepes and serve at once.

For lemon crepes:

FILLING

2 8-ounce packages cream cheese, softened
⅔ cup sugar
juice of 1 lemon
1 tablespoon grated lemon rind
1 tablespoon light rum

SAUCE

½ pound butter
¼ cup sugar
½ cup lemon juice
1 tablespoon grated lemon rind

Beat cream cheese in electric mixer on medium speed until fluffy. Gradually add sugar, and beat again. Stir in lemon juice, rind, and rum. Fill crepes with filling, roll up, and tuck the ends under the seam side.

Melt butter in a large skillet. Add sugar and stir and heat until sugar melts. Stir in lemon juice and rind. Add the crepes and heat about 2 minutes, turning crepes over in the sauce. Add a little Grand Marnier if desired.

Lemon crepes are wonderful after seafood, but strawberry crepes can't be beat. Choose from the two, or if you're energetic, make both and let the guests choose.

MINT JULEPS
28 SERVINGS

For each mint julep you will need 1 ounce of mint syrup and 2 ounces of the best bourbon you can buy. Mix the syrup and bourbon in a silver julep cup, add crushed ice, and stir until the glass frosts. Garnish with fresh mint.

MINT SYRUP

2 cups water
2 cups sugar

juice of 6 lemons
3 cups mint

Wash the mint thoroughly. Stir sugar and water together in a saucepan and boil for 10 minutes. Pour hot syrup over the mint and let it steep several hours. Add the lemon juice. Strain and pour into glass jars and refrigerate. Use as needed, as this will keep for several weeks.

A trip to the South is not complete without at least one mint julep. Only problem is, one calls for two.

CLAM PUFFS

SERVES 8 TO 10

1 7-ounce can minced clams
1 8-ounce package cream cheese
1 teaspoon onion, grated

dash Worcestershire sauce
½ loaf thinly sliced bread, cut in rounds

Cream the cheese and add the clams, which have been well drained. Add seasonings and mix well. Toast bread rounds on one side only. Cover the untoasted side of the bread rounds with the clam mixture, not skimping when you cover. Place under broiler until lightly browned and puffed. Serve immediately. These can be fixed well ahead and refrigerated before cooking.

As the seasons change, so do our menus at Hamilton Hall. We tend to serve lighter food in the summer, but as fall arrives we go to heavier food and maybe some dishes that we have not had in a while. As more new items hit the grocery-store shelves, it causes us to update our old recipes to include some time-saving steps, as long as we don't compromise on quality and taste.

EGGS BENEDICT

SERVES 8

8 English muffins, split, buttered, and lightly toasted
16 slices ham, lightly browned in butter

16 eggs, soft poached
1 recipe béarnaise sauce (see page 87)
parsley, paprika, salt, and pepper to taste

If you are making this dish for a crowd, the poaching of the eggs could cause a problem, but not to worry. Do it this way: Place the egg in the shell in simmering water for 10 seconds before breaking it. This sets the egg just a bit. Then break the egg into a cup and slip it carefully into enough simmering liquid to cover it. I usually poach in half white wine and half water or lightly salted water with 1 tablespoon vinegar added for each quart of water used. Simmer for 3 to 4 minutes or until the white is just firm and a film has formed over the yolk. Remove the egg from the water with a slotted spoon and place in a bowl of cold water to stop the cooking process. Remove the egg from the water and trim off uneven edges with a sharp knife if you desire. Eggs may be prepared ahead, as many as you like, kept in the cold water, and refrigerated for several hours. Before serving, place the eggs in hot, salted water for about 30 seconds or until heated through. Drain them well on paper towels before serving. Place toasted muffin halves on a plate with ham slices on top, then eggs and cover with béarnaise sauce. Sprinkle with paprika and top off with a piece of parsley. Doing eggs in this manner, you can serve large groups of people with relative ease.

This is my absolute favorite dish for brunch, but since it does contain a high level of fat, it now has to be for a special occasion—but, my, how I look forward to it.

BANANA NUT BREAD

SERVES 8 TO 10

½ cup butter
1 cup sugar
2 eggs, beaten
1 cup plain flour
1 cup cake flour
1 teaspoon baking powder
½ teaspoon baking soda

¼ teaspoon salt
1 teaspoon vanilla
3 ripe bananas, mashed
1 tablespoon buttermilk
3 tablespoons brown sugar
½ cup nuts, chopped

Cream butter and sugar. Add eggs. Add dry ingredients, which have been sifted together. Add vanilla and bananas. At last, stir in quickly the buttermilk, brown sugar, and nuts. Bake in a greased loaf pan about 1 hour at 350°.

Don't ask me about the last-minute addition of the buttermilk and brown sugar. I don't know why I do it that way, except it just gives it a wonderful flavor and you taste the brown sugar immediately, especially if you eat the bread while it is hot from the oven, as we do. Actually, I just add a handful of brown sugar, but since all hands are different sizes, I had to come up with an amount.

CHEESECAKE SQUARES

42 SQUARES

1 cup all-purpose flour
¼ cup brown sugar, firmly packed
1 cup nuts, either walnuts or pecans,
    chopped
½ cup butter, melted
2 8-ounce packages cream cheese, softened

1¼ cups sugar
1 teaspoon vanilla
3 eggs, lightly beaten
2 cups sour cream
⅓ cup sugar
1 teaspoon vanilla

Combine the flour with the brown sugar and nuts. Pour the melted butter over this. Mix well and press into the bottom of a 13″ x 9″ x 2″ flat glass baking dish. Bake at 350° for 15 minutes. While this is cooking, beat the cream cheese with the sugar and vanilla. Add the beaten eggs and mix well. Remove crust from oven and pour this mixture into it and bake an additional 20 minutes. While this is cooking, mix the sour cream with the ⅓ cup sugar and another teaspoon vanilla. Remove from oven and spoon this over the baked filling and return to the oven for 5 to 8 minutes. Cool, cover, and refrigerate. Cut into squares and decorate each square with a slice of strawberry or a piece of kiwi or a fresh raspberry, or some other kind of fruit.

This is nice for a ladies' tea, on a buffet of finger desserts, which we do often, or as a midmorning treat. The nuts in the crust make it special.

Mississippi Caviar

Cheesy Zucchini Soup

Corn Sticks

Carolyn Stewart's Italian Cream Cake

◆

Tangy Broccoli Salad

Creole Oysters on Kaiser Rolls

Southern Pecan Pie

◆

Fresh Spinach Salad with Honey Mustard Dressing

Vegetable Lasagna

Bread Pudding with Whiskey Sauce

◆

Panned Catfish with Two Sauces

Baked Red Potatoes

Zucchini Fans

Southern Peach Cobbler

◆

Bloody Good Aspic

Shrimp and Wild Rice Casserole

Quick Rolls

Mississippi Mud Cake

◆

Lettuce and Vegetable Layered Salad

Muddy's Spaghetti

Quick Herb Bread

Peanut Butter Pie

◆

Best-Layered Mexican Dip

My Seafood Gumbo

Tennessee Spoon Bread

Black Forest Cheesecake

An Outrageous Affair

❖

Whether it be Saturday lunch for the family or friends in on Sunday night, these recipes are intended for informal weekend occasions and they are outrageously good.

MISSISSIPPI CAVIAR

SERVES 10

2 1-pound cans black-eyed peas, drained
  and rinsed
1 medium red onion, chopped
¾ cup salad oil
½ cup cider vinegar

1 clove garlic, mashed, or ½ teaspoon
  garlic seasoning
½ teaspoon salt
freshly ground pepper to taste
dash of Tabasco

After draining and rinsing peas, place in a bowl with chopped onion. In separate bowl, mix the oil, vinegar, garlic, salt, Tabasco, and pepper. Pour over the peas and onions. Mix thoroughly. Store in a covered container in refrigerator for at least 12 hours before serving. Put in a glass bowl with a slotted spoon for dipping onto saltine crackers. Y'all come on down to the Deep South and have some caviar—"Mississippi Style." That really is what we say when we mean "all of you," and this really is what we serve on occasion at cocktail parties. Both are traditions in the Deep South.

CHEESY ZUCCHINI SOUP

SERVES 4 TO 6

3 medium zucchini, washed, ends
   trimmed, unpeeled, and grated
3 medium-size carrots, peeled and grated
1 stick butter
1 onion, chopped
¼ cup flour

2 13½-ounce cans chicken broth lo salt
1 cup Monterey Jack cheese, grated
1 cup half-and-half
¾ teaspoon salt
¾ teaspoon white pepper

Sprinkle zucchini liberally with salt and let drain in a colander for 20 minutes. Squeeze water from zucchini. Melt butter in medium-size saucepan and sauté onions for a minute, then add zucchini and carrots and cook for about 3 or 4 minutes. Stir in flour and, stirring constantly, let it bubble for a few minutes. Add chicken broth in a slow, steady stream, stirring all the while. Then add grated cheese and stir while it melts. Add half-and-half and season to taste with the salt and white pepper. Add the amount a little at a time until you have it to your liking, as some chicken broth is very salty. You will have 4 servings if you are using this soup as the main course on a Sunday night.

This soup is a great favorite of ours. Served with a salad or sandwich, it is a great luncheon choice also. If dieting, you can use 2 percent milk, liquid Butter Buds, and low-fat cheese, but of course, it isn't nearly as tasty. But then what is, without the real thing?

CORN STICKS

1 cup cornmeal
1 tablespoon flour (optional)
½ teaspoon salt
½ teaspoon baking soda
1 teaspoon baking powder

1 egg, slightly beaten
1 cup buttermilk
2 tablespoons bacon drippings or
  vegetable oil

Brush corn-stick pans with the bacon drippings or oil, leaving the excess oil in the pan to get hot. Set the oven at 425° and put the pan in the oven to get hot. Sift the meal, flour, salt, baking powder, and baking soda. Add the egg and buttermilk to the dry ingredients. Pour the hot drippings from the pan into the mixture and stir well. Spoon into the hot pan and bake for about 20 minutes.

If you are looking for sugar in this recipe, you won't find it, because true southerners never add sugar to their corn bread and they always use white cornmeal. I do not add the flour but some like a little. Of course, we use cast-iron black pans and I think we have one in every style they make.

CAROLYN STEWART'S ITALIAN CREAM CAKE

SERVES 12 TO 16

CAKE

½ cup butter, softened
½ cup vegetable shortening
2 cups sugar
5 eggs, separated
2 cups flour

1 teaspoon baking soda
1 cup buttermilk
1 teaspoon vanilla
1 cup coconut
1 cup nuts, chopped

Cream the butter and shortening; add sugar gradually and cream well. Add the 5 egg yolks, one at a time, beating constantly at a medium speed. Sift together the flour and baking soda and add this alternately to the creamed mixture with the buttermilk.

Add vanilla, coconut, and nuts. Beat the egg whites in a separate bowl until stiff and fold them into the cake mixture. Pour into 3 8-inch cake pans that have been greased and floured. Bake at 350° for 25 minutes, or until done. Cool and frost.

FROSTING

1 8-ounce package cream cheese
½ cup butter
1 teaspoon milk
1 teaspoon vanilla

1 1-pound box confectioners' sugar, sifted
1 11-ounce jar of pineapple or strawberry ice cream topping (optional)

Beat together the cream cheese and butter. Add the sugar and milk and vanilla. Put the ice cream topping between the layers, but not on top. Frost sides and top with frosting. You can add ½ cup additional nuts to the frosting, if you like. You do not have to use the topping; you can just use the frosting between the layers.

This is a terrific recipe from a gal who really knows how to bake. She uses the pineapple topping, but I have tried the strawberry (since that is my favorite) and that works well also.

TANGY BROCCOLI SALAD

SERVES 6 TO 8

2 bunches broccoli, or enough to make
   4 cups broccoli flowerets
¾ cup raisins
1 cup fresh mushrooms, sliced

⅓ cup purple onion, chopped
8 slices bacon, cooked very crisp, drained
   of grease, and crumbled

Blanch the broccoli in boiling water for a few seconds until it turns a beautiful bright green. Immediately plunge it into ice water to stop the cooking. Drain well on paper towels. Store in the refrigerator until time to serve. Then combine with other ingredients and toss with the dressing just before serving.

DRESSING

1 jumbo egg
½ cup sugar
½ teaspoon dry mustard
1½ teaspoons cornstarch
¼ cup cider vinegar

¼ cup water
¼ teaspoon salt
2 tablespoons butter, brought to room
   temperature
¾ cup Hellmann's mayonnaise

Bring to a boil the vinegar, water, and salt. Whisk the egg, sugar, mustard, and cornstarch, which you have mixed together into the vinegar mixture. Cook at medium heat until it thickens, stirring constantly. Remove pan from stove and stir in butter. Cool a little bit, add the mayonnaise, and stir. You will need to make this ahead and refrigerate it so that it will be well chilled before you pour it on the salad. Check to see if you want to add additional salt and a little pepper.

Be prepared for lots of compliments when you serve this. We use lots of broccoli and this is yet another way to serve it. Serving it with a one-dish meal, as we are doing in this menu, it takes the place of both a salad and a vegetable.

CREOLE OYSTERS ON KAISER ROLLS

SERVES 10

½ cup butter
1 cup flour
2 quarts shucked oysters
1 teaspoon Tabasco
¼ teaspoon basil
1 clove garlic, crushed
½ teaspoon paprika
3 tablespoons Worcestershire sauce

1 tablespoon Accent
2 tablespoons lemon juice
2 tablespoons ketchup
2 tablespoons sherry
¼ cup parsley, finely chopped
1 tablespoon onion, grated
salt and pepper to taste

Melt butter in large saucepan and slowly add flour. Brown the flour slowly, so as not to scorch, and cook until coffee-colored. Heat the oysters in their own juice in another pan, just until the edges begin to curl. Drain off the juice from the oysters. Return the oysters to the refrigerator until just before serving time. Heat the juice from the oysters and add it to the roux, stirring constantly while adding the liquid slowly. Stir well and add all the other ingredients. Cook sauce in top of a double boiler for 20 minutes. Just before serving add the oysters, which you have brought to room temperature, to the very hot liquid. Heat through and serve on toast shells (see below). You can make the sauce ahead and refrigerate the sauce and oysters separately until ready to reheat in double boiler.

These oysters can be served on patty shells, but I like to use the kaiser rolls, which I have dug the center out of to form a basket. Brush the inside with butter and toast in a slow oven. This looks pretty and tastes great with the oysters.

SOUTHERN PECAN PIE

SERVES 6 TO 8

CRUST

1 cup all-purpose flour
⅓ cup Crisco

pinch salt
3 tablespoons ice water

Sift the flour and salt together. Add the Crisco and cut into the flour with a pastry blender until a crumbly mixture is formed. Do not mix too fine. Add the water, a little at a time, until the pastry holds together in one lump. Roll out on a floured board and place in the bottom of pie pan. Press crust into pan, fitting it closely so that no air bubbles remain underneath. Flute the edges.

FILLING

¼ cup butter
1 cup sugar
3 eggs, well beaten
1 cup dark corn syrup

1 teaspoon vanilla
1 cup pecans, chopped
½ cup black walnuts, chopped (optional)

Beat butter with sugar. Stir in eggs and mix thoroughly. Add the corn syrup, vanilla, and nuts. Put in unbaked pie shell and bake at 350° for 40 to 50 minutes.

A few extra pecan halves placed in a pattern on top makes this pie pretty. Sure, the black walnuts are optional, but if you try it, I bet you will like it.

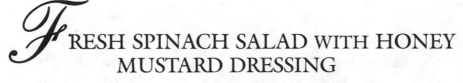

FRESH SPINACH SALAD WITH HONEY MUSTARD DRESSING

SERVES 8 TO 10

1 pound fresh spinach, washed and large
stems removed

1 head curly green leaf lettuce, washed and
pulled apart and each leaf pulled into
pieces

8 ounces fresh mushrooms, washed and
sliced

2 11-ounce cans mandarin oranges, drained
and chilled

1 pint strawberries, washed, hulled, and
sliced if large

1 purple onion, sliced in thin rings

1 slice bacon for each person to be served,
cooked, well drained, and crumbled

DRESSING

2 cups Hellmann's mayonnaise
½ cup honey
½ cup mustard

splash of cider vinegar
onion salt to taste
red pepper flakes to taste

Mix together the mayonnaise, honey,
and mustard. Splash in the vinegar
and sprinkle in the onion salt and red pepper
flakes. The flakes make the dressing pretty as
well as adding a little hot flavor, so add a little
and then taste for seasoning. Refrigerate and
serve cold.

Hand-lay the spinach and lettuce pieces
on individual serving plates. Then add
mushroom slices on top, along with the
orange sections and strawberry slices. Top
with red onion slices. Just before serving,
pour salad dressing over all in a swirling
motion so that some of the orange and red
from the fruit show through. Crumble bacon
on top. You may need more spinach,
depending on the amount of waste you have.

This salad is beautiful in a large glass bowl for
the buffet table. Just mix all salad ingredients
together and crumble bacon on top, with the
salad dressing in a bowl on the side.

Can you imagine serving this salad to 800
people! We did just that for Congressman
G. V. "Sonny" Montgomery's twenty-fifth
Congressional Anniversary Celebration. Since
at that time he was senior ranking member of
the House Armed Services Committee and
chairman of the House Veterans Affairs
Committee, it was fitting that this event take
place at our local naval air station—in the jet
hangar, no less. There was no kitchen, no
water, no stove, no refrigerator, no ice, and
we would have twenty minutes in which
to serve 800 people. At first I said no, it

couldn't be done; but then I love a challenge and now I can look back on it with a great deal of pride. Several offices were taken over for improvised kitchens, "water buffaloes" straight from Desert Storm were brought in to supply water for the coffee urns and drinking.

All the food was cooked at Hamilton Hall and transported the morning of the luncheon in National Guard trucks to the hangar. We brought the pecan-walnut tarts (the recipe for pecan pie found on page 30 was adapted to tarts) frozen, so that they would not spoil before lunchtime, and we brought the salad dressing iced down in ice chests. The salad was made by our staff, early in the morning, and refrigerated in the mess hall at the base and trucked down to the hangar right before serving time. The tables were all set the day before with linen cloths and napkins, china, and silverware, but after they were set we learned that pigeons roosted in the rafters at night, so we covered the tables with huge sheets of plastic that we quickly confiscated from a local dry cleaner. The shrimp and wild rice (see page 41) was easily kept warm in our buffet pans—but how could I reheat the cooked beef tenderloin without overcooking it? I found a huge oven in the hangar that is used to melt down metal parts, and right before the meat was to go on the buffet lines, all the pans of meat were put on a large steel plate that slid into the oven. The heat in that oven was tremendous and it wasn't possible to see what was happening inside; you think I wasn't nervous when I saw that plate disappear with my meat, and all those people sitting out there waiting to be served. Oh my, how I wished to be back at Hamilton Hall with my big gas ovens. Did we get it served on time? How about four buffet lines and fifteen minutes. Would I do it again? Not on your life!

VEGETABLE LASAGNA

SERVES 8 TO 10

1 medium eggplant, peeled and cut into medium-size cubes
8 ounces fresh mushrooms, sliced
½ cup olive oil
1 32-ounce jar Prego spaghetti sauce with mushrooms
1 red bell pepper, sliced in strips lengthwise
1 cup carrots, chopped
4 small cloves garlic, mashed
2 tablespoons onion, finely chopped
1 teaspoon oregano
½ teaspoon salt

¼ teaspoon white pepper
10 drops Tabasco
2 cups cottage cheese
½ cup Parmesan cheese, grated
2 eggs, lightly beaten
2 tablespoons fresh parsley, chopped
2 cups zucchini, thinly sliced
1 8-ounce package shredded mozzarella cheese
1 6-ounce package shredded Monterey Jack cheese
1 8-ounce box lasagna noodles, cooked
¼ cup Parmesan cheese, grated

Sauté eggplant and mushrooms in olive oil. Add spaghetti sauce, peppers, carrots, garlic, onion, oregano, salt, pepper, and Tabasco. Simmer 25 minutes. While this is cooking, mix the cottage cheese with the eggs, Parmesan cheese, and parsley. Mix the mozzarella and Jack cheeses together. Put a layer of the cooked noodles in the bottom of a 9" x 13" x 2" glass baking dish; then a layer of the spaghetti sauce; a cup of the zucchini; and half of the cottage cheese mixture; then half of the mozzarella and Jack cheeses; another layer of noodles, sauce, zucchini; the other half of the cottage cheese mixture; and the other half of the cheeses; then top it off with the last of the spaghetti sauce. Bake at 400° to get it hot through for about 15 minutes, then cover it with foil and bake for 45 minutes, reducing the temperature to 350°. Remove the foil, sprinkle with the last of the Parmesan cheese, and bake an additional few minutes until the cheese browns.

Don't be intimidated by the long list of ingredients. Once the chopping is done, it's a snap. Of course, don't try to make it for a hundred people, as we did one day at Hamilton Hall. We chopped and added and stirred and mixed, and we never wanted to see this dish again, until we sat down to eat the leftovers and we decided it was well worth it.

BREAD PUDDING WITH WHISKEY SAUCE

SERVES 10

8 cups day-old french bread cubes
4 cups milk
4 eggs, beaten
1½ cups sugar
8 tablespoons butter, melted

1 cup whipping cream
½ teaspoon salt
1 tablespoon vanilla
1 cup raisins

Scald milk. Place bread in a large bowl and pour the milk over it. After it has soaked a few minutes, mix together with your hands until well mashed. Add the eggs, sugar, whipping cream, salt, and butter and stir. Add vanilla and raisins and mix well. Grease a long, heavy baking pan with butter and pour in the bread pudding. Place this pan in another pan that has boiling water in it, about halfway up the pudding pan. Bake in medium oven, at about 350°, for about 45 minutes. We serve it warm with whiskey sauce.

SAUCE

½ cup butter
2 cups sugar

4 eggs, beaten
10 tablespoons whiskey

Melt the butter and add the sugar, and cook in the top of a double boiler until sugar is dissolved. Put a little in the bowl with the beaten eggs and stir. Return to the mixture in pan; stir at a low heat until thickened. You do not want your egg to curdle. Remove from the stove and let the sauce cool. Add whiskey. Top individual servings with the sauce and run under the broiler for a few minutes until top is crusty.

Nothing is more satisfying on a cold day than bread pudding for dessert. They call it ''soul food'' for good reason; it satisfies the very soul.

PANNED CATFISH WITH TWO SAUCES

SERVES 6 TO 8

or orange roughy

1 tablespoon salt
1 teaspoon onion powder
1 teaspoon paprika
½ teaspoon cayenne pepper
½ teaspoon black pepper
½ teaspoon white pepper
2 tablespoons Cavender's Greek seasonings
1 tablespoon Accent

1 teaspoon Tony Chachere's seasonings
1 teaspoon garlic powder
½ to 1 cup milk
1 beaten egg
1 cup flour
6 to 8 catfish fillets
vegetable oil
½ cup pecans, chopped and dry roasted

Mix together seasonings, sprinkle some on fillets and combine the rest with the flour. Combine milk and egg. Dip fillets in flour, then in egg mixture, then back in flour. Panfry in oil in cast-iron skillet, then put in 350° oven for 10 to 15 minutes.

BUTTERED MEUNIÈRE SAUCE

1 cup seafood stock (if not available, use chicken stock)
¾ teaspoon minced garlic
¼ pound unsalted butter, divided in half

2 tablespoons flour
¼ cup Worcestershire sauce
¼ teaspoon salt

In a large saucepan, combine the stock and garlic. Bring to a boil and simmer 2 to 3 minutes. In a small saucepan, melt half the butter, add the flour, and whisk until smooth. Add to hot stock gradually, stirring constantly. Reduce heat to simmer. Add remaining butter and whisk until melted. Add remaining ingredients and cook until sauce thickens.

PECAN BUTTER SAUCE

4 tablespoons unsalted butter, softened
½ cup pecans, chopped and dry roasted
2 tablespoons onion, finely chopped

1 teaspoon lemon juice
¼ teaspoon minced garlic
½ teaspoon Tabasco

Put all ingredients in food processor until creamy, about 2 or 3 minutes.

When ready to serve, put meunière sauce on plate, top with fish fillet, then pecan butter sauce. Sprinkle on a few of the dry roasted pecans.

B. B. Archer, one of the city's leading architects by profession, is a fantastic cook who does wonderful things with seafood. He originated this recipe, which was intended for orange roughy, but any firm, white fish will do. Of course, you could just use the meunière sauce with catfish you have dipped in egg and then in crushed Ritz crackers and baked at 350° until crunchy. The Greek seasoning is all you would need before the egg wash, with a little melted butter poured over the fish before baking.

These seasonings should be available nationally. Cavender's All Greek Seasoning is a blend of salt, pepper, cornstarch, garlic, oregano, beef-flavored base, parsley, and five other spices not listed. If not available, write to S-C Seasoning Company, Box 1296, Harrison, Arkansas 72501.

Tony Chachere's Creole Seasoning contains salt, red pepper, and other spices. Their address is Creole Foods, P.O. Box 1687, Opelousas, Louisiana 70571, 1-800-551-9066. You need these seasonings in your pantry for anytime you are cooking seafood.

BAKED RED POTATOES

SERVES 6 TO 8

2½ pounds small red potatoes, halved
4 tablespoons olive oil
½ teaspoon salt, or to taste

½ teaspoon pepper, or to taste
½ teaspoon Hungarian paprika

Place potatoes in a large bowl and pour olive oil over them and toss. Then place in a baking pan, cut side down. Sprinkle with the salt, pepper, and paprika. Bake for 30 to 35 minutes at 425° until potatoes are tender and underside is brown and skins are crisp.

An easy and delicious way to enjoy potatoes.

UCCHINI FANS

SERVES 8

8 small zucchini, washed
flour
garlic salt and pepper to taste

butter
lemon juice
parsley

Parboil zucchini in salted water until just barely tender. Drain carefully and then dry with paper towels or clean tea towel. Refrigerate. When cold, slice lengthwise, 3 or 4 times, to within an inch of the end; then press gently with your hand to make them open like a fan. Sprinkle lightly with flour, garlic salt, and pepper. Sauté in butter to a delicate brown on both sides. Remove zucchini and add butter to the butter in the frying pan, heat, and pour over the zucchini, if you desire. Sprinkle with finely chopped parsley and lemon juice and serve.

This makes a beautiful addition to any plate. You may not want the butter poured on top of the zucchini with this particular menu, as you have the sauces on the fish.

SOUTHERN PEACH COBBLER

SERVES 10

PASTRY

1 cup self-rising flour
½ teaspoon salt

⅓ cup Crisco
4 teaspoons milk

Stir together the flour and salt. Cut in the Crisco with a pastry blender until a crumbly mixture is formed. Add the milk a little at a time until you have a stiff dough. Roll out on a floured board.

FILLING

8 large peaches, peeled and sliced, or
**   2 packages frozen peaches**
½ cup water
2 tablespoons self-rising flour
pinch of salt

1½ cups sugar
½ cup butter, melted
2 teaspoons lemon juice
¼ teaspoon nutmeg

Put peaches in a large saucepan and pour the water over them. Cook until tender at medium heat. In a separate bowl, stir together the flour, salt, and sugar. Add this to the cooked peaches. Mix together and add the melted butter, lemon juice, and nutmeg. Pour half of the peaches into a 9" x 13" x 2" pan. Cut some strips from the prepared pastry that has been rolled out, and push the strips down into the peaches. Pour in the rest of the peaches and top with strips of the pastry in a latticework design. Bake at 350° for about 40 minutes or until top is brown.

All cobblers need a sprinkle of sugar and bits of butter scattered over the top. This makes the crust a beautiful brown and also makes it crunchy. This recipe comes from my sister-in-law, Peggy Gross, in Charlotte, North Carolina. She is a wonderful cook and has always shared her recipes with me.

BLOODY GOOD ASPIC

SERVES 10

2 10½-ounce cans Campbell's beef broth
2 32-ounce bottles Mr. and Mrs. T bloody
  mary mix
1 17-ounce can English peas, drained
1 8½-ounce can artichoke hearts packed in
  water, drained and cut in fourths
1 cup green pepper, diced
1 cup celery, diced

½ cup fresh green herbs, chopped (can be
  one or a mixture of parsley, marjoram,
  thyme, green onions, chives, chervil, but
  do not use tarragon)
¼ cup Worcestershire sauce
big splash of cider vinegar
big splash of Tabasco
5 envelopes unflavored gelatin

Sprinkle gelatin over one can of beef broth in a saucepan. Bring to a boil and dissolve completely. Set aside. Mix all other ingredients together and add gelatin mixture and stir carefully. Can be put in a large ring mold or individual molds.

Serve on curly leaf lettuce with a salad dressing of half mayonnaise and half sour cream. Sprinkle with Hungarian paprika. The flavor of tarragon does not lend itself to the other ingredients.

SHRIMP AND WILD RICE CASSEROLE

SERVES 8

1 6-ounce box of Uncle Ben's long grain and wild rice with seasonings, cooked according to directions
1½ pounds raw shrimp, cleaned but not cooked

1 10¾-ounce can cream of mushroom soup, undiluted
1½ cups sharp cheddar cheese, grated
1 tablespoon Worcestershire sauce
salt and pepper to taste

Combine all ingredients. Place in a greased, flat glass casserole. Bake at 350° for 30 minutes. Add a few drops of Tabasco if not serving with a spicy salad, like the Bloody Good Aspic.

Nice meal when you are in a hurry, that is if you clean the shrimp the day before.

QUICK ROLLS

SERVES 10

2 cups self-rising flour
2 tablespoons sugar
¼ cup melted Crisco

1 package dry yeast
½ cup warm water
⅔ cup buttermilk

Mix flour with sugar. Add melted shortening and mix well. Dissolve yeast in warm water. Add dissolved yeast and buttermilk to flour mixture. Roll out on a floured board. Roll out to ⅜ inch, cut with cutter, and place in a well-greased pan. Allow rolls to rise for at least an hour. Bake at 400° for about 10 minutes.

This recipe came about by accident. Once we actually forgot about making rolls. About one hour before time to serve, someone thought about it, and we came up with this quickie. It worked and no one seemed to know the difference except the cleanup crew, as I got into such a hurry that I spilled flour everywhere.

MISSISSIPPI MUD CAKE

SERVES 12

CAKE

1 cup butter
½ cup cocoa
4 eggs, slightly beaten
2 cups sugar
1½ cups all-purpose flour

pinch salt
1½ cups pecans, chopped
1 teaspoon vanilla
1 7-ounce jar marshmallow cream

Melt butter and cocoa together. Remove from heat. Stir in the sugar and eggs. Mix well. Add flour, salt, nuts, and vanilla and stir together. Spoon into a greased 9" x 13" x 2" pan and bake at 350° for 35 to 40 minutes. Spread with marshmallow cream. When cool, spread with frosting.

FROSTING

1 1-pound box confectioners' sugar
1 stick butter
½ cup cocoa

½ cup evaporated milk
1 teaspoon vanilla

Beat ingredients together.

This is a Deep South recipe that makes you forget all about calories.

LETTUCE AND VEGETABLE LAYERED SALAD

SERVES 12

1 large head iceberg lettuce, shredded
1 cup celery, chopped
½ cup green bell pepper, chopped
½ cup red onion, chopped
1 10-ounce package frozen baby green
   peas, thawed

white pepper
1½ cups Hellmann's mayonnaise
1 tablespoon sugar
2 cups extra sharp cheddar cheese, grated
12 strips bacon, fried, drained, blotted,
   and crumbled

Put lettuce in the bottom of a 9″ x 13″ x 2″ glass baking dish. Sprinkle the celery over the lettuce; then the green pepper; then the onion; then the peas. Sprinkle with white pepper. Spread the mayonnaise evenly over the vegetables very carefully so as not to disturb them and seal the salad with the mayonnaise on the sides of the dish. Sprinkle the sugar over the mayonnaise. Sprinkle the cheese over all. Cover with the plastic wrap and refrigerate. It is best to do this the day before serving. Cook the bacon the day you are serving the salad, and crumble over each serving. Cut in squares.

We don't serve just plain green salads at Hamilton Hall, as we feel you can get them anywhere. This has the extra perk of being able to be made ahead, and you won't have to worry about the salad wilting.

$\mathcal{M}$UDDY'S SPAGHETTI

SERVES 5

¼ cup olive oil
1 medium onion, chopped
1 medium green bell pepper, chopped
3 ribs celery, chopped
8 ounces fresh mushrooms, sliced
1 14-ounce can stewed tomatoes
1 6-ounce can tomato paste
⅓ cup ketchup
¼ cup chili sauce
1 cup hot water
½ teaspoon chili powder (more, if desired)
1 tablespoon Worcestershire sauce

dash Tabasco
1 bay leaf
parsley, to taste
1½ teaspoons salt, or to taste
freshly ground pepper
¼ cup or more olive oil
1 pound ground chuck
1 3-ounce can Armour potted meat
1 2¼-ounce Underwood deviled ham
2 cups Parmesan cheese, freshly grated
1 8-ounce package thin spaghetti

Put ¼ cup olive oil in an iron skillet. Sauté the onions, peppers, celery, and mushrooms until limp, but do not brown. Transfer to a large, heavy boiler. Add tomatoes, tomato paste, ketchup, water, chili sauce, chili powder, salt, Worcestershire sauce, Tabasco, and bay leaf. Allow this to boil down somewhat and then add parsley. While this is cooking down, mix the ground chuck, potted meat, and deviled ham with salt and freshly ground pepper. Shape into meatballs, roll in freshly grated Parmesan cheese, and brown on all sides in the same iron skillet with additional oil, starting with ¼ cup. Drain on paper toweling. Add the meatballs to the sauce and simmer for one hour. Cook the spaghetti according to package directions. When done, pour into a colander and drain; scald with hot water.

Drain again and mix the spaghetti in with the sauce. Serve with freshly grated Parmesan cheese.

This recipe was given to me by a dear friend, Natalie Wood, who is a wonderful cook and loves pasta. She says this serves six hungry people, but there were only three of us for lunch and we just about finished it off, so safely say four or five. "Muddy" was Natalie's grandmother. You may think that name strange, but it's not as strange as what they called their cook, whom they dubbed "Yes." Her name was really Rachael, but every time "Muddy" would call Rachael she would answer "Yes," and so Natalie thought that was her name. Since she called her "Yes," everybody else did, too—and so goes the South.

QUICK HERB BREAD

SERVES 8

½ cup butter, softened
1 teaspoon dried parsley flakes
¼ teaspoon dried oregano, crumbled
½ teaspoon dill weed

1 clove garlic, finely minced
freshly grated Parmesan cheese
1 loaf french bread

Mix together the softened butter and herbs. Cut bread into 1-inch diagonal slices. Spread mixture on each slice. Put bread slices back together, loaf-style, and place on a large piece of foil. Sprinkle cheese over the loaf. Wrap and bake at 400° until hot. Open foil and allow bread to sit in hot oven for a few minutes to crisp the edges a bit.

Our downstairs guest bath is between the kitchen and an outside door. One night, a guest came into the kitchen and asked where the facilities were. Bob, who was in the kitchen working, replied, "Next door, sir." In a few seconds, we heard the back door open and close—Bob looked at me and I at him. He quickly ran out the outside door and retrieved the gentleman, who I suppose thought we meant literally at the neighbors', or maybe he thought he was headed for a "long ago" Mississippi outhouse.

PEANUT BUTTER PIE

SERVES 6 TO 8

CRUST

1 8- or 9-inch pie shell (see page 30)
½ cup crunchy peanut butter

¾ cup confectioners' sugar, sifted

Mix together the peanut butter and sugar with your fingers until smooth.

Spread half of this in bottom of pie shell and bake at 400° until crust is done.

FILLING

2 cups milk, scalded
¼ cup cornstarch
⅔ cup sugar

2 tablespoons soft butter
5 egg yolks
1 teaspoon vanilla

Scald milk in top of double boiler. Blend the cornstarch and sugar well and then add butter and egg yolks. Pour a little of the milk into these ingredients and then return it to the rest of the milk in the top of the double boiler. Cook, stirring constantly, on a

very, very low heat until mixture thickens. Cool slightly and add vanilla.

When done spread filling over peanut butter crust.

TOPPING

5 egg whites

10 tablespoons sugar

Whip whites until soft peaks form, then slowly add sugar and whip until stiff. Spread meringue over pie filling. Top with bits of the other half of the peanut butter mixture and bake for 15 to 20 minutes until golden brown.

A real treat for peanut butter lovers. This recipe comes from my good friend Todd Sanderford, who is always there when I need him. At one time, he was in the food service business, and he literally had to get down on his knees and beg a baker that he knew for this recipe. I'm so glad he did.

BEST-LAYERED MEXICAN DIP

SERVES 8

1 16-ounce can refried beans with green
    chilis
3 ripe avocados, peeled and chopped
2 tablespoons lemon juice
dash of Worcestershire sauce
dash of Tabasco
dash of garlic powder
salt and pepper to taste

1½ cups sour cream
1 package taco seasoning mix
2 tomatoes, peeled and diced
4 green onions, white and green parts,
    chopped
8 ounces cheddar or Monterey Jack cheese,
    or both, grated
pitted black olives for garnish

Spread beans on bottom of a 9″ x 13″ flat glass casserole. Purée the avocados with the lemon juice, Worcestershire, Tabasco, garlic powder, salt, and pepper. Spread the avocado mixture over the beans. Mix the taco seasoning with the sour cream. Pour a layer of this over the avocado. Layer the tomatoes, green onions, and then the cheese. Make sure some green and red show through the cheese to make it attractive. Garnish with sliced black olives. Don't forget the corn chips or tortilla chips. You can certainly make this ahead, but keep it refrigerated.

We have so many requests for this, that I felt I had to include it in this book. If you are pressed for time, or if you can't find any ripe avocados, use two cans of frozen guacamole dip. Or, if you like, just leave off the avocado layer.

MY SEAFOOD GUMBO

SERVES 8

5 strips of bacon, fried, or enough to make
    5 tablespoons bacon drippings
6 tablespoons flour
1 large bunch green onions, chopped
1½ cups celery, chopped
2 cloves garlic, finely chopped
1 28-ounce can tomatoes, chopped
1 8-ounce can tomato sauce
6 cups water
1 tablespoon salt

1 teaspoon black pepper
1 tablespoon parsley flakes
2 teaspoons Creole seasoning
8 drops Tabasco
1 pound frozen cut okra, thawed
3 pounds shrimp, shelled, deveined, and
    cut into pieces if large
1 pound crabmeat, picked through to
    remove any shells or bones
3 tablespoons Worcestershire sauce

Put bacon drippings in large, heavy, dutch oven–type pan. Slowly add flour and cook over medium to low heat, stirring constantly for about 30 minutes until very dark. Be careful not to scorch. If you do scorch the mixture, you will have to start all over again. Add onion, celery, and garlic and sauté for a very few minutes. Add canned tomatoes, tomato sauce, water, and all seasonings except Worcestershire and simmer for an hour. Add okra and simmer for another hour. Add shrimp and crabmeat and simmer for 15 minutes. Add Worcestershire and stir. Taste for seasonings. Serve over rice.

Be sure and eat the bacon while making the roux—it gives you something to do.

TENNESSEE SPOON BREAD

SERVES 6 TO 8

2 cups milk, scalded
½ cup cornmeal, sifted
3 tablespoons melted butter

1 teaspoon salt
½ teaspoon baking powder
3 eggs, separated

Pour the cornmeal into the pan with the scalded milk, stirring constantly, over medium heat. By the time it comes to a boil, it will be thick and you are ready to remove it from the stove. Add the butter, salt, and baking powder and stir. Cool. Beat the egg yolks and add them in thirds to the meal mixture, stirring well after each addition. Beat the egg whites to a soft peak and fold into the meal mixture. Pour into a well-buttered 1½-quart baking dish and bake uncovered in a 375° oven for about 30 minutes, or until set but not dry. A round glass dish works best. Serve immediately, buttered or not.

Spoon bread is a southern treat my grandmother made for me as a child. I called this Tennessee Spoon Bread because many places outside the South have never heard of it. My grandmother was the youngest of eleven girls who were well known throughout Nashville for their southern cooking. I can't say they were "gourmet" cooks, nor would their dishes have fit that category. The Cain girls were famous, however, for getting every dish in the kitchen dirty while they were cooking. It has been said that I definitely take after my grandmother in that category.

BLACK FOREST CHEESECAKE

SERVES 12

CRUST

1½ cups chocolate wafer crumbs
⅓ cup sugar

6 tablespoons butter, melted

Using the food processor, grind the chocolate wafers into crumbs. Add the sugar and butter to the crumbs and blend.

Pat the crumb mixture onto the bottom and halfway up the sides of a buttered 10-inch springform pan.

FILLING

3 8-ounce packages cream cheese, softened
1 cup sugar
4 eggs
⅓ cup heavy cream

1 teaspoon vanilla
6 ounces semisweet chocolate, melted
1 16-ounce can pitted dark sweet cherries, drained and patted dry

Cream the cheese and add the sugar, beating all the while. Add the eggs, one at a time, beating well after each addition. Add cream and vanilla, beating until light. Melt the chocolate in a heavy skillet on low heat and stir into the cake mixture. Pour about half of the batter on top of the crust in prepared pan. Top with the cherries. Spoon remaining cake mixture evenly over the cherries. Bake at 350° for 45 minutes. Cool and then cover lightly and chill. When ready to serve, remove sides from pan and garnish with whipped cream and additional cherries, if desired.

Under the best of circumstances, accidents do happen at Hamilton Hall. Once we were entertaining a famous Hollywood singer and dancer who was in town to star in a local production. We were excited that she was coming for lunch, along with local dignitaries, and had everything planned down to the last detail. We were well pleased with the way things seemed to be going, up until Bob was passing a tray of wine and he just couldn't get the guest of honor's attention to offer her a glass, as she was talking. He really got her attention, though, when the last glass on the tray slid, hit the rim of the tray, and poured down her dress. What can you say, except, "I'm so sorry, let me get a towel."

Crunchy Chicken Casserole

Cranberry Chutney

Broccoli with Almond-Olive Sauce

Our Famous Popovers

Carl's Cookies

◆

Barbecued Beef Short Ribs

Artichoke Potato Salad

Boiled Slaw

Ree's Biscuits (see page 6)

Mammy's Fried Apple Pies

◆

Chicken and Rice Casserole

Cranberry Knockout

Fresh Asparagus (see page 90)

Black Russian Cake

◆

Pork Loin Roast with Sour Gravy

Fried Corn

Spinach Casserole

Corn Sticks (see page 26)

Tomato Relish

Old-Fashioned Strawberry Shortcake

◆

Meat Loaf

Real Mashed Potatoes

Turnip Greens

Green Tomato Casserole

Mississippi Corn Bread

Quick Fudge Pie

❖

A Family Affair

❖

Some of these recipes are family favorites, some are included by requests from my children, and some are for my young married friends, who are constantly calling and asking, How do you fry corn? or, How do you cook turnip greens? One thing you can count on: they have all proved to be timeless in enjoyment.

CRUNCHY CHICKEN CASSEROLE

SERVES 8

6 ounces medium-size noodles, cooked and
  drained
2 whole chicken breasts, cooked and diced
  to make 2 cups
½ cup celery, chopped
½ cup onion, chopped
½ cup pimiento, chopped

½ stick butter, melted
½ teaspoon salt
¼ teaspoon pepper
1 10¾-ounce can cream of celery soup
½ cup milk
1 cup American cheese, grated
potato chips, crushed

While noodles are draining, mix chicken with vegetables. Add noodles and pour melted butter over noodles, then mix all together. Mix undiluted soup with milk and cheese in a medium-size saucepan and heat slowly, stirring until warm. Add salt and pepper. Mix with noodle mixture and pour into a buttered 2-quart flat casserole. Top with crushed potato chips, using as many as you like but making sure you cover the entire top. Bake at 425° for 30 minutes.

I am very fortunate in that my husband likes casseroles. Many men don't. He has a gluten intolerance, so we use only DeBoles artichoke flour pasta. Even if we didn't have to use DeBoles for health reasons, we wouldn't use anything else because it has such a clean taste and never gets gummy.

CRANBERRY CHUTNEY

SERVES 8

1 12-ounce package fresh cranberries
2 cups sugar
1 cup water
1 cup orange juice
1 cup golden raisins

1 cup walnuts or pecans, chopped
1 cup celery, chopped
1 medium apple, chopped
1 tablespoon orange peel
1 teaspoon ginger

Heat cranberries, sugar, water, and orange juice in a 3-quart saucepan until boiling. Reduce heat and simmer for 15 minutes. Remove from heat. Add additional ingredients. Cool and refrigerate.

Buy lots of cranberries in the fall and keep in the freezer so that you can make this all year.

Teaching adult education classes for the Meridian public school system has been such fun. I'm quite sure that I have learned more than my students. This recipe came from one of my most faithful students, Susan Murray, who took every class that I offered during her husband's tour of duty with the Meridian Naval Air Station. When they were transferred, the local navy officers wives' club gave her a farewell party at Hamilton Hall. I cried.

BROCCOLI WITH ALMOND-OLIVE SAUCE

SERVES 6

½ cup butter, melted
1 clove garlic, crushed
2 tablespoons lemon juice
1 2¼-ounce can ripe olives, drained and
 sliced

½ cup sliced almonds
2 small or 1 large bunch fresh broccoli,
 trimmed of large stalks
salt

Melt butter in small saucepan. Add crushed garlic and stir. Add lemon juice and olives. Let stand 30 minutes. Reheat before serving and add sliced almonds. Cook broccoli in boiling, salted water in flat pan until barely done. Drain well and spoon sauce over. Since broccoli is available year-round, we count on it a lot. We have never used frozen, but use it if you must.

Several years ago, my mother moved from Nashville to make her home at Hamilton Hall. She sets an absolutely beautiful table and molds butter into flowers and bells, but her claim to fame is playing dress-up. Can you imagine ringing our doorbell and having a bunny rabbit or Santa Claus answer the door?

OUR FAMOUS POPOVERS

SERVES 6

3 eggs
1¼ cups milk, at room temperature
1¼ cups all-purpose flour

pinch of salt
oil

Hand-beat eggs with a whip or hand mixer until lemon colored and foamy. Add milk and stir until well blended but do not overbeat. Add flour and salt all at once. Hand-beat until foamy and smooth on top. Grease popover or muffin tins lightly, but well. Fill popover tins with batter or if using muffin pans, fill every other hole. Bake at 450° for 15 minutes, reduce heat to 350° for 30 minutes. When ready to serve, remove them from the tin with a sharp knife and serve hot. Caution: Do not open oven door to check popovers or they will fall. If cooking more than one tin of popovers, remove first tin quickly and close oven door immediately. (This recipe was developed before popover pans, hence the instruction to use every other hole of the muffin tins, so when they rise they will not touch each other.)

This recipe comes from my friend Janice Eatman, who told me this story:

In 1957, she and her husband went to Dallas for their first big shoe market. There were no shopping malls—downtown Dallas was it. They stayed at the Baker Hotel, and the flagship Neiman-Marcus was just a block away. In 1957, that was some store, and there she bought her first cookbook other than Betty Crocker's—Helen Corbitt's first cookbook, which is now out of print. When Neiman-Marcus opened in Atlanta, Janice and her husband were there for lunch, and she remembers a lady standing at the end of the cashier counter. The cashier was handing out this popover recipe. Janice took one and told the cashier about her first Helen Corbitt cookbook, and how it helped her develop an interest in good food. The lady who was standing there, just looking around, asked her if she had any questions about the popover recipe, so Janice asked her if she should or should not heat the pans. The lady answered, "Don't heat, don't peek, don't overbeat." With that she turned and walked off. Janice asked the cashier who that lady was, and she answered that it was Miss Helen Corbitt herself. I love this story, because I, too, am a big Helen Corbitt fan and have every cookbook that she ever wrote and also the *Helen Corbitt Collection*, which was published after her death, but it does not contain this recipe.

CARL'S COOKIES

MAKES 6 DOZEN

1 cup butter
1 cup sugar
1 egg, beaten
2 cups plain flour

½ teaspoon baking powder
½ teaspoon baking soda
pinch salt
1 teaspoon vanilla

Beat butter and sugar until creamy. Add the egg. Sift the flour, baking powder, baking soda, and salt and add to creamed mixture. Add vanilla.

FOR CHOCOLATE CHIP COOKIES: Add 1 cup chocolate chips and 1 cup pecans, chopped.

FOR NUT COOKIES: Add 1 cup of your favorite nuts, chopped.

FOR ALMOND COOKIES: Omit vanilla and add 1 teaspoon almond extract.

Chill the dough for at least 2 hours. Roll out in small balls and flatten with a fork on a greased cookie sheet. Bake at 350° for 10 minutes.

Running an inn can be very frustrating at times. This won't work, that won't work; this is broken; how can we do this without spending a fortune? When we are at our wits' end, we call Carl. He can find a way to do anything. Among other things, he hung a piece of stained glass on a window that is located on a stairway landing where the ceiling is about fifteen feet high and there is no place to put a ladder. He sat down on the steps and studied it a while, then said he was ready. I couldn't watch, but when I came back it was done. This dear friend, Carl Sanderford, can also cook. Try this simple cookie recipe with all its variations and you will agree.

BARBECUED BEEF SHORT RIBS

SERVES 4

4 pounds beef ribs
1 teaspoon salt
⅛ teaspoon pepper
2 lemons, sliced
1 large onion, sliced
2 cups water
1 cup tomato ketchup

¼ cup Worcestershire sauce
¼ cup vinegar
1 tablespoon celery seed
¼ cup brown sugar
1 teaspoon chili sauce
dash Tabasco

Lay ribs in a large, flat glass baking dish and sprinkle with salt and pepper. Put lemon slices and onion slices on top. Bake at 450° for 30 minutes. Combine the remaining ingredients in a saucepan and bring to a boil. Pour over ribs and continue baking at 350° for 1½ hours.

When you think of the South, you think of pork barbecue. But this recipe attests to the fact that beef short ribs can be just as delicious.

ARTICHOKE POTATO SALAD

SERVES 4 TO 6

2 tablespoons lemon juice
1 tablespoon dijon mustard
1 clove garlic, mashed
salt and pepper to taste
⅓ cup olive oil
1 14-ounce can artichoke hearts, well
   drained and chopped in wedges

⅓ cup black olives, coarsely chopped
   (optional)
2 tablespoons fresh parsley, chopped
1 tablespoon green onions, minced
1 to 1½ pounds new potatoes, scrubbed,
   cut in pieces, boiled, and drained

In a large bowl, whisk together the lemon juice, mustard, garlic, and salt and pepper. Add oil in a steady stream, whisking all the while. Beat until well combined. Add the artichoke wedges, black olives, parsley, and green onions. Toss the mixture. Add the potatoes, while they are still warm, to the artichoke mixture. Chill and serve.

A little different slant on potato salad, but if you are fond of artichokes you will find this very good.

BOILED SLAW

SERVES 8

1 large head of cabbage, about 2½ pounds, shredded
1 large onion, finely chopped
1 green pepper, finely chopped
1 cup Puritan oil

1 cup cider vinegar
1 cup sugar
1 teaspoon celery seed
1 tablespoon salt

Put shredded cabbage in bottom of large bowl. Layer onions and bell peppers on top of cabbage. Sprinkle sugar over top of vegetables. Do not stir. Place remaining ingredients in a saucepan and bring to a boil. Pour over vegetables while it is still hot. Do not stir. Refrigerate for at least 8 hours. Stir before serving.

You will enjoy this slaw, especially since it doesn't contain any mayonnaise, and it will also keep in the refrigerator for about a week.

The lawn at Hamilton Hall has never looked more beautiful than it did the day of our daughter's wedding. Jan and I got up quite early and sat on the porch rockers. It was very cloudy and drizzling rain. We drank our coffee and looked at each other, knowing full well what the other was thinking. We were having an outside reception after a high noon wedding, and the tents were up, blowing softly in the breeze, with their colored tulles of blue, pink, green, and purple beckoning. The caterers arrived at eight o'clock and by then it was looking much worse outside, but we carried on—it was much too late to change anything. By the time we arrived at the church, it was raining; but when she stepped out the side door of the church to go around to walk down the aisle, the sun came right out and beamed almost as brightly as she did. The yard at Hamilton Hall was filled with blooming flowers, brought out in pots just in time so the rain wouldn't damage them. A jazz group played on the patio and spring-colored cloths adorned the round tables all over the yard. The food was wonderful: seafood pasta, fresh salmon, pâtés, cheeses, fresh fruit with chocolate fondue, breakfast tortillas, chicken kabobs, and hot small reuben sandwiches, among other things. The groom's cake was an array of cheesecakes—praline, coconut, and strawberry—and the wedding cake, well, each tier was a different flavor inside: Italian Cream (the recipe for which can be found on page 27), raspberry, and orange kiss. It was quite an affair, with Max (Jan's dachshund) parading around the yard in his new tuxedo made especially for the occasion. This was a wedding that truly reflected the Deep South and its traditions.

MAMMY'S FRIED APPLE PIES

SERVES 8

1½ cups dried apples
3 cups water
¼ cup honey or sugar to taste
2 tablespoons lemon juice
½ teaspoon grated lemon rind
½ teaspoon cinnamon
¼ teaspoon salt
⅛ teaspoon nutmeg

3 cups all-purpose flour, sifted
1 teaspoon salt
1 cup Crisco
6 tablespoons cold water
Puritan oil for frying
butter
confectioners' sugar

Place apples in the water in a saucepan, cover, and bring to a boil. Reduce heat and simmer until apples are tender and the water has been absorbed. Remove from the heat and stir until smooth. Add the honey, lemon juice, rind, cinnamon, nutmeg, and salt. Stir well. Cut the Crisco into the flour and salt until it resembles coarse meal. Sprinkle with the cold water and mix until pastry is formed. Divide into 2 balls. Roll out one ball on a lightly floured surface and cut out with a 5-inch cutter. Place 1 tablespoon apple filling on half of the circle. Dot with butter. Fold over and dampen edges and press edges with a fork to seal. Continue with all pastry, keeping pies covered with a damp cloth until ready to cook. Heat 2 cups of oil in a large skillet to 375° and fry pies a few at a time until golden brown, turning once or twice while frying. Drain on heavy paper and dust lightly with confectioners' sugar.

"Mammy and Pappy" was what Bob affectionately called his grandparents. Mammy was a wonderful cook, and Bob remembers her fried apple pies, among other things, with great reverence. I don't really have her recipe, and I'm quite sure that hers were much better than mine. Of course, her work was much harder, since she had to pluck the apples, dry them, chop wood for the stove and get the fire good and hot, and use lard left from hog killing to fry them in. She cut out her pies with the top of a large baking powder can, and I'm not too sure whether that was five inches or not; anyway she lived to be eighty-five, so I don't suppose the hog lard hurt her. When our first grandchild came along, our children asked us what we wanted him to call us. Bob won out with the name Pappy, but somehow Mammy never made it for me. I am Gingone to my wonderful grandchildren, Jay and Elaine, and they love my fried pies.

CHICKEN AND RICE CASSEROLE

SERVES 6 TO 8

1 cup white long grain rice
1 10¾-ounce can cream of mushroom soup
1 10¾-ounce can cream of chicken soup
1 10¾-ounce can cream of celery soup
1 soup can water

¼ cup or more of dry sherry
seasoned salt to taste
8 skinless, boneless chicken breast halves
2 tablespoons margarine, melted
pepper to taste

In a medium-size bowl, rinse the cup of rice. Add to it the three soups, water, sherry, and seasoned salt. Pour into a large, flat 3-quart buttered casserole. Lay the chicken breasts on top of the rice. Sprinkle with pepper and pour the melted margarine over them to prevent drying. Bake uncovered at 250° for 3 hours.

A wonderful dish for Sunday morning. It can cook while you are at church with no fear of its overcooking.

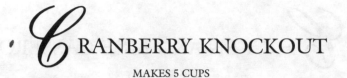

CRANBERRY KNOCKOUT

MAKES 5 CUPS

1 16-ounce package of raw cranberries,
   washed and picked over
1½ to 2 cups sugar

1 10-ounce jar orange marmalade
juice of 1 to 1½ lemons
½ cup (or more) black walnuts, chopped

Put washed cranberries with sugar in a dutch oven–type pan. Bake in oven at 350° for 1 hour. Remove from oven and let cool a few minutes and add marmalade, nuts, and lemon juice. Mix thoroughly and put in a jar or jars with a tight-fitting lid. Refrigerate. Will keep in refrigerator for at least 6 months.

How could this recipe not be good, with two of my very favorite ingredients—cranberries and black walnuts? The amount of sugar and lemon juice will depend on how sweet you like your cranberries and how big the lemons are.

BLACK RUSSIAN CAKE

SERVES 12

CAKE

1 18½-ounce box deep chocolate cake mix
½ cup salad oil
1 4½-ounce package instant chocolate
    fudge pudding and pie filling

4 eggs, at room temperature
¾ cup strong coffee
¾ cup combined Kahlua and crème
    de cacao

Combine cake mix, salad oil, pudding mix, eggs, coffee, and Kahlua and crème de cacao mixture in a bowl. Beat about 4 minutes at medium speed of mixer or until smooth. Spoon into a well-greased bundt pan and bake at 350° for 45 to 50 minutes. Remove from pan when cool. Punch holes in cake with ice pick and spoon topping over cake.

TOPPING

1 cup sifted confectioners' sugar
2 tablespoons strong coffee

2 tablespoons crème de cacao

Combine ingredients and mix well.

This is a good example of using modern conveniences such as a cake mix and still coming up with a wonderful product. Although we use very few mixes, this is good enough to make the cut.

PORK LOIN ROAST WITH SOUR GRAVY

SERVES 6 TO 8

1 6-pound pork loin roast with bone in
salt
pepper
garlic salt

2 to 3 tablespoons flour
1 to 1½ cups water and cider vinegar
 combined

Have your butcher crack the bones on the back side of the roast for easy carving. Wipe the roast with a clean damp cloth and season the roast liberally with the salt, pepper, and garlic salt. Place the roast, bone side down, on a rack in a roasting pan. Bake at 300° for at least 3 hours, uncovered. The secret of this roast is in the slow cooking for a long period of time. The fat on the top of the roast should be very brown and crusty by the time you remove it from the oven. Lift the roast onto a platter to keep warm, and remove the rack from the bottom of the pan. Place the roasting pan (I use a large iron skillet) on the top of the stove, and on medium heat, slowly stir the flour into the pan. The amount of flour you will need will depend on the amount of grease you have in the pan from the roast. You may need to pour off some of the grease before browning

the flour, depending on how fat the roast was. Slowly brown the flour until it is a dark, golden brown but be careful not to burn it. This will take a few minutes, but the slow browning is very important. Then, pour in the water and vinegar, stirring constantly. If you need more water and vinegar to make it thinner, just keep your proportions of an equal amount of water and vinegar. Salt and pepper to taste.

Refusing to be intimidated by the wave of low-fat cooking, I am including this method of cooking pork loin roast, which was used by my grandmother. I remember well how excited the houseguests were when they came into my grandmother's dining room and found that succulent piece of meat with gravy and great bowls of candied sweet potatoes.

FRIED CORN

SERVES 6

8 ears of fresh corn, shucked and silked
salt and pepper
2 to 3 tablespoons bacon drippings

3 tablespoons butter
water

Hold the ear of corn in the palm of your left hand at a 45° angle, stem end down in the bottom of a large boiler. Cut the corn off the cob using a very sharp small knife or an apple peeler held in your right hand, starting at the top of the ear and going downward, and barely capping the top of the kernels. Rotate the ear of corn and cut in this manner until you have capped the whole ear. Then go around the ear of corn with the knife and scrape the corn, with the milky substance falling into the pan with the kernel tops. When you have finished with all the ears, heat the bacon drippings in a large skillet, keeping the amount of drippings in proportion to the amount of corn you have been able to "milk" from the ears. When the grease is hot, add the corn and sauté for a few minutes. Then add water, about equal to the amount of corn. Add salt and pepper to taste, and 3 tablespoons of butter and let cook until thick. If you have trouble getting it to thicken, stir a little of the corn into a tablespoon of cornstarch and return it to the skillet. This would be caused by immature corn.

A few years ago, Bob and I went back to a little wide spot called Burns, Tennessee, where his grandparents had lived. To get to his grandparents' "place," we drove on a country lane, crossing an open creek in the road three times, finally arriving at a trail leading up a hill to their house. There at the top of the hill we saw a three-room log cabin still standing, covered with vines and unattended bushes. On the back porch hung a well-remembered bucket with no bottom and on the floor of the porch sat the rim and sides of a dishpan. In the kitchen, Bob showed me where the woodstove had stood that his grandmother had cooked on. She had had no sink, no water spigot, no electricity, no refrigerator, no food processor, but she turned out some of the finest food that has ever been eaten. Her fried corn was like smooth satin. She didn't have to buy a "six-pack," as we do, and hope that four of those six ears would be good. She went to the field and plucked her corn, shucked it, but when she capped the kernels, she threw the caps out to the chickens and used only the scrapings for her wonderful dish. Later in the day, as I stood in the old graveyard and gazed down at the marker that read MINDA HAMILTON HOLLAND, I thought of the hard life this dear woman had lived, but then wouldn't she be pleased that her grandson and granddaughter-in-law wanted to return to catch a glimpse of her life?

SPINACH CASSEROLE

SERVES 6 TO 8

2 10-ounce packages of frozen chopped
   spinach, thawed
6 tablespoons butter, melted
1 cup saltine cracker crumbs
2 cups milk

3 eggs, beaten
1 onion chopped
salt to taste
1 cup sharp cheddar cheese, shredded
   (optional)

Drain spinach, squeezing out all the water. Pour melted butter over the spinach and stir. Pour the milk over the cracker crumbs and onions. Add to the spinach mixture. Add the eggs. Salt to taste and stir. Bake in a buttered casserole, round or flat. Place casserole in a larger pan and fill the outer pan with boiling water halfway up the sides of the casserole. Bake at 350° for 40 minutes. Remove from oven. Sprinkle cheese over top and return to oven for 5 minutes.

This is one of my mother's recipes that we have enjoyed so much, both for the family and entertaining. Sometimes for a buffet she will bake it in a ring mold and fill the center with small, buttered new potatoes sprinkled with paprika. It is a favorite with both the ladies and the men. As you can see, it can be easily doubled.

TOMATO RELISH

MAKES 5 PINTS

15 large tomatoes, scalded, peeled, and
   chopped
3 medium onions, chopped
2 green bell peppers, chopped
1½ cups white vinegar

2½ cups sugar
2 tablespoons salt
2 tablespoons pepper
2 tablespoons pickling spice, tied in
   cheesecloth or jelly bag

Dissolve the sugar in the vinegar and mix with the vegetables in a large pot. Put the pickling spice bag down into the vegetables, add salt and pepper, and cook over medium to low heat for 2 hours. Pour the relish into 5 hot, sterilized pint jars and seal. Then give the jars a hot-water bath for 15 to 20 minutes. Cool and store.

This easy relish cannot be surpassed. It is a product of a fine cook here in the Deep South, Bobbie McLemore.

OLD-FASHIONED STRAWBERRY SHORTCAKE

SERVES 8

2 cups all-purpose flour
4 teaspoons baking powder
½ teaspoon salt
⅓ cup sugar
dash nutmeg
½ cup Crisco
½ cup whipping cream

¼ cup water
1 quart fresh strawberries, washed, hulled,
  and mashed
sugar for strawberries, according to taste
  or sweetness of berries
butter
1 cup whipping cream, whipped

Sweeten mashed berries and refrigerate. Sift together the flour, baking powder, salt, nutmeg, and sugar. Cut in the Crisco with pastry blender. Stir in the cream and water that have been mixed together. Roll out on a floured board to about an inch thickness and cut with a round cutter to desired size. Bake on an ungreased cookie sheet at 450° for about 15 minutes. Split biscuits when placing on individual serving plates, butter them, and cover bottom layer with sweetened strawberries. Cover with top half of biscuit, more strawberries, and whipped cream. Garnish with a strawberry on which you have left the stem.

The basic dessert. Who can refuse?

MEAT LOAF
SERVES 5

1½ pounds ground chuck
1 small onion
salt and pepper to taste
1 slice white bread, pulled into crumbs
1 egg, lightly beaten
2 tablespoons milk

1 8-ounce can tomato sauce
½ cup water
2 tablespoons vinegar
2 tablespoons brown sugar
2 tablespoons yellow mustard

Mix together the meat, onion, salt and pepper, bread crumbs, egg, milk, and half the can of tomato sauce. Mold into a loaf and bake at 350° for 35 minutes. Pour off juice in pan. Blend the other half can of tomato sauce with water, vinegar, brown sugar, and mustard. Heat in a saucepan and then pour over the meat loaf and return it to oven at 300° for another 30 minutes, basting occasionally with the sauce.

There have been only five days that Hamilton Hall had to completely close; it was due to the cat-in-residence. Thomas is a big, gray part-Persian, of whom, to say the least, my mother is overly fond. Unbeknownst to our daughter, Jan, he rode back to her home in Jackson in the trunk of her car. It was Christmas night at 7:30 when we learned of this adventure, and of course, upon the trunk's opening, Thomas had leaped out and run like crazy. At 10:30, ninety miles from home, we were in a hopeless situation, driving around neighborhoods and shopping centers in a city of 250,000 calling "Thomas!" After all, it was time for him to be rocked to sleep and he had not yet had his supper. We stayed for two days, doing everything possible, but to no avail. Three days later, Bob and I drove back for a last desperate search, and just as it was getting dark, in a wooded area behind Jan's apartment building, I shook a can of Pounce and gave one last dinner call, "Everybody come on!" Out of his hiding place, a muddy ditch, walked a tired and hungry Thomas. When we put Thomas in Mother's arms, we reminded her of the reward she had offered, but the best reward was getting life back to normal at Hamilton Hall.

REAL MASHED POTATOES

SERVES 4 TO 5

1½ pounds baking potatoes (about 2 large Idahos)
½ cup milk, warmed

½ cup heavy cream, warmed
6 tablespoons butter, melted
salt and pepper to taste

Peel the potatoes and cut them into large pieces. Cover with cold water, bring to a boil, then turn down the heat and boil gently until tender when you poke them with a fork. Be very careful not to let them cook too long. When they are just done, drain them immediately and put them back into the hot cooking pan and let them dry. I turn the heat off on the stove but let them sit back on the eye. Drying them out makes for fluffier potatoes. Beat the potatoes; it doesn't matter how you beat—with an electric mixer, which I use, a wooden spoon, or a wire whisk. Add the warmed milk and cream. Cold milk will make potatoes gummy. Add the milk gradually and then add the butter. If you add the milk and butter all at once it will make the potatoes watery and loose, so be sure to add them gradually. The amount of milk and cream you need will vary with the type of potato you use. You probably won't need quite as much as I've indicated. The potatoes should be creamy and they will thicken slightly when you stop beating them. These are absolutely delicious reheated in the microwave at about 60 percent power. They never lose their consistency. Don't forget the salt and pepper.

Homemade mashed potatoes with a well of melted butter in the center is perhaps the soul food of Americans—but who makes them anymore? So it might take a little time; think about these wonderful potatoes next time you pour hot water over those little buds and shove a prepackaged meal into the oven. You're missing a lot!

TURNIP GREENS

SERVES 6

2 to 3 bunches of turnip tops (3 pounds)
1 ham hock or ¼ pound boiling bacon
water

salt to taste
pinch baking soda

Carefully wash and pick over the greens, removing tough stems. Wash in several waters to be sure to remove all grit. Bring water and seasoning meat to a boil and simmer for about 20 minutes. You will want enough water barely to cover the greens. Add the greens, and cook at a low boil until greens are tender (about 1 hour). Stir often, seasoning to taste. When you think the greens are about done, add a pinch of baking soda. Meat may be removed and cut up into greens. You may like a mixture of mustard greens or collards with your greens. The "pot likker" is the seasoned liquid in which the greens are cooked, and many southerners enjoy a "sop" with their cornbread.

My friend Barbara Larkin tells me of a friend, Betty Sue, who moved up North. One day at the market she was delighted to see a big, beautiful bunch of turnip greens. At the checkout counter the cashier proceeded to twist off the greens from the turnips and threw the greens in the trash and the turnips in the grocery bag. Betty Sue, who stood dumbfounded, screamed, "Give me back my greens, I don't want the turnips," much to the consternation of the checker, who thought the greens were just waste material that would take up room in the grocery bag. Betty Sue made him get every piece out of the trash; after all, she had paid for them, and she thought that checker was totally uninformed.

GREEN TOMATO CASSEROLE

SERVES 4 TO 6

2½ pounds green tomatoes, cut in ½- to
   ¼-inch slices
1 tablespoon sugar
salt and pepper to taste
¾ cup fresh bread crumbs
3 tablespoons butter

½ teaspoon oregano
¼ teaspoon basil
¼ teaspoon thyme
sprinkle of garlic powder
⅓ cup Parmesan cheese
3 tablespoons butter

Arrange tomato slices slightly overlapping in a lightly oiled flat casserole. Sprinkle with sugar and salt and pepper. Lightly brown bread crumbs in butter and combine with the oregano, basil, and thyme and a little garlic powder. Sprinkle crumb mixture over the tomatoes. Top with cheese and dot with butter. Bake at 350° about 45 minutes.

Be careful not to overbake this wonderful dish or the tomatoes will get limp. I like the tomatoes best about ¼-inch thick and they take less time to bake, but it is always hard to get ¼-inch slices when the knife slips.

MISSISSIPPI CORN BREAD
SERVES 6

1 tablespoon bacon drippings or
   Puritan oil
1 egg, slightly beaten
¾ cup plain white cornmeal
1 teaspoon baking powder

½ teaspoon salt
1 cup buttermilk
½ teaspoon baking soda
1 teaspoon water

Preheat oven to 500°. Put drippings or oil into a medium-size (8½ inches across the top) cast-iron skillet or equivalently sized pan. Preheat pan. Add the meal, baking powder, and salt to the egg. If you want to use a corn bread mix instead of these 3 ingredients, that is fine. Add the buttermilk and stir. Dissolve the baking soda in the water and mix into the meal. This is a very thin batter. Pour some of the hot drippings from the preheated pan into the batter and stir. Pour into the hot skillet and bake for about 20 minutes.

If you would like to add some cracklings to this batter before placing it in the oven, it would make some mighty fine eating with those turnip greens. Add about ¾ cup for this amount of meal. For those of you who do not know what they are, cracklings are crisp little pieces of pork skin.

QUICK FUDGE PIE

SERVES 6 TO 8

2 squares bitter chocolate
1 stick butter
1 cup sugar
scant ¼ cup flour

pinch of salt
2 whole eggs, beaten
½ cup chopped walnuts

Melt butter with chocolate in saucepan over very low heat. Remove from heat and add sugar that has been mixed with the flour and salt. Then add eggs and beat well. Stir in nuts. Pour into a buttered 8-inch pie pan and bake at 325° for 30 minutes.

This is delicious topped with ice cream. Strawberry or black cherry are great choices, but peppermint is my favorite. You can make your own peppermint ice cream by crushing an 8-ounce package of Bob's Old Timey Pure Sugar Sticks and blending with a half gallon of softened vanilla ice cream and refreezing.

Ladies' Luncheon

Fresh Fruit with Poppy Seed Dressing

Chicken Breasts with Shrimp Champagne Sauce

Celebration Rice

Broccoli with Almond-Olive Sauce (see page 56)

Charlotte Russe

◆

Formal Dinner Party

Hot Artichoke Dip

Little Macs

Avocado Mousse with Creamy Shrimp Dressing

Beef Tenderloin with Sautéed Mushrooms and Béarnaise Sauce

Wild Rice with Almonds

Fresh Asparagus

"Home-Maid" Rolls

Cold Lemon Mousse Cake with Hot Raspberry Sauce

◆

Buffet Dinner Party

Daube Glacé

Three-Tier Cheese Pâté (see page 105)

Shrimp Remoulade

Artichoke Chicken

Carrots and Pistachios and Cointreau

French Chocolate Mousse

❖

A
Scrumptious
Affair

❖

Every party we have at Hamilton Hall is special. These menus were designed for such occasions, and the recipes are the most often requested and we feel they are "special" in themselves. You might find them a little time-consuming (what party isn't?) but certainly not difficult. Enjoy!

FRESH FRUIT WITH POPPY SEED DRESSING

SERVES 12

Lay any or all of the following fruits out on a tray or combine in a beautiful crystal bowl.

fresh pineapple, cut into bite-size pieces

strawberries, washed and hulled and sliced, if large

cantaloupe, made into balls with a melon baller

honeydew melon, made into balls with a melon baller

watermelon, cut in bite-size pieces with a crinkle cutter

If using as individual salads, hand-lay this salad on a curly green leaf of lettuce.

blueberries, washed

raspberries, washed

peaches, peeled and cut in long, thin pieces with a little lemon juice squeezed on

white, red, or black grapes, seedless and washed

star fruit, cut in slices

kiwi, cut in slices

DRESSING

¾ cup sugar

1 teaspoon salt

1 teaspoon dry mustard

⅓ cup cider vinegar

1 cup Puritan oil

1½ tablespoons grated onion

2 tablespoons poppy seeds

Using your blender, whirl the dry ingredients together. Pour in the vinegar and whirl. Slowly add the oil while it is whirling. When thick, pour into a bowl and stir in the onion and the poppy seeds. Serve this very cold.

Nothing is more beautiful on a buffet or more welcomed than a gorgeous arrangement of fresh fruit. Serve the dressing from a separate dish because some like their fruit plain. We learned the hard way when we were doing a graduation luncheon for a group of girls and prepared their fruit salads by topping them off with the poppy seed dressing. No one ate her salad but the mother of the honoree and the hostess; the girls just picked out the fruit that didn't have the dressing on it. Oh, how we hated to throw out that beautiful fruit!

CHICKEN BREASTS WITH SHRIMP CHAMPAGNE SAUCE

SERVES 8

4 chicken breasts, halved, skinned, and
  boned
salt and pepper to taste
flour
4 tablespoons butter
¾ pound fresh mushrooms, sliced
1½ pounds shrimp, peeled, deveined but
  uncooked

4 green onions, sliced
3 tablespoons lemon juice
1 teaspoon salt
¾ cup water
6 tablespoons flour
1 teaspoon instant chicken bouillon
1½ cups half-and-half
¾ cup champagne

Lightly salt and pepper chicken breasts and dust with flour, shaking off any excess, and sauté breasts in butter until very light brown. Place in a long glass casserole and put in a 250° oven to finish the cooking, while you make the sauce. Sauté the mushrooms in butter and set aside. In a bowl, combine the shrimp, green onions, lemon juice, and salt. In a large skillet, over medium heat, sauté the shrimp mixture until shrimp turns pink. Remove shrimp with a slotted spoon and set aside. In a small bowl, combine the water, flour, and bouillon. Stir this mixture into the hot liquid in the skillet in which you have cooked the shrimp. Stir until well blended. Gradually add the half-and-half and champagne. Cook, stirring constantly, until mixture thickens and comes to a boil. Stir in mushrooms and shrimp. Correct seasonings—you may desire to add more lemon juice or salt. Serve over chicken breasts, with a sprinkle of paprika and a lemon twist.

This is a favorite selection for bridesmaids' luncheons. Not only does it make a beautiful plate, it is also a delicious treat that is very well received.

CELEBRATION RICE

SERVES 8

½ cup butter, melted
1 cup carrots, chopped
1 cup onions, finely chopped
1 small to medium bell pepper, chopped

1 cup celery, finely chopped
3 10¾-ounce cans chicken broth
1½ cups raw rice
½ cup fresh parsley, chopped

To the melted butter in skillet, add the carrots, onions, celery, and bell pepper. Sauté for 4 to 5 minutes, but be careful not to brown. Heat broth in separate saucepan. Pour broth into a 2-quart baking dish; add the rice and stir for about 2 minutes. Add sautéed vegetables. Cover and bake at 350° for about 45 minutes. Before serving, toss rice with parsley or sprinkle parsley over each serving.

Rice goes so well with this menu because of the wonderful champagne sauce over the chicken. The sauce with a bit of this rice is divine.

Lobster has always been one of my very favorite foods, so I was very delighted when a friend decided to have fresh lobsters flown in from Maine for his wife's birthday celebration at Hamilton Hall. Air freight delivered them on the afternoon of the party, as planned. I looked at the shipping cartons for about an hour before deciding I simply must check on the lobsters before cooking time. When I opened them up, much to my horror, they were all dead. By that time, it was five o'clock; the party was at seven and the whole dinner was planned around the fresh lobsters. I quickly called the host. What to do? At 6:30, he and his son appeared at the door with cartons and cartons of lively lobsters, which they had gathered from every market in the area that handled fresh seafood. They had bought every lobster they could find—everyone had a different size—but every guest at that party had lobster. My mouth watered with the serving of each one, knowing this was one time the cook didn't get to eat.

CHARLOTTE RUSSE

SERVES 8

1 envelope unflavored gelatin plus
   1 teaspoon
½ cup cold water
4 eggs, separated
¾ cup sugar
2 cups milk

pinch of salt
sherry to taste
2 tablespoons sugar
1 cup whipping cream, whipped
2 dozen ladyfingers
½ cup sliced almonds, toasted

Sprinkle gelatin over cold water. Set aside. Combine egg yolks, salt, and sugar and beat until light. Scald milk in top of double boiler and pour over the sugar and egg mixture. Return to top of double boiler and cook until mixture coats a wooden spoon; remove from heat and add gelatin and cool. Add sherry to taste. Beat egg whites until very stiff, adding the 2 tablespoons sugar while beating. Fold the custard into the egg whites. Fold in the whipped cream. Line a large glass bowl or the sides and bottom of a 9-inch springform pan with the ladyfingers. Pour in custard mixture. Top with almonds. Refrigerate for several hours before serving.

A southern favorite that is timeless.

HOT ARTICHOKE DIP

SERVES 16

2 14-ounce cans artichoke hearts, drained
1½ cups Hellmann's mayonnaise
½ cup sour cream
2 cups Parmesan cheese, freshly grated

½ teaspoon garlic and parsley salt
juice of ½ lemon
Tabasco to taste

Squeeze all the water out of artichokes, then mash. I use a wooden potato masher. Mix with the rest of ingredients. Bake at 350° for about 30 minutes, or until hot and beginning to brown. Use melba-toast rounds for dipping on your favorite cracker; Triscuit is a good choice. Serves 16 to 20 as an appetizer or you may halve the recipe for a party for 8. If you wish to make this low fat, simply use no-fat sour cream and mayonnaise.

This recipe, one of our favorites, was given to me by a fellow lover of good food—Billie Jo Braden—many years ago. She and her husband, Bill, got married at Hamilton Hall in 1982 and now have two beautiful children. With so many weddings at our home, we have been blessed with lots of grandchildren, or so we feel.

ITTLE MACS

MAKES 40

1 loaf thinly sliced white bread
1 small onion, very finely chopped
3 tablespoons butter (no substitution)
¾ pound mushrooms, washed and finely
   chopped
2 tablespoons flour

¾ teaspoon Tabasco
¾ teaspoon salt
¼ teaspoon black pepper
½ cup half-and-half
melted butter for brushing
butter and oil for frying

Cut each slice of bread into four rounds with small round cutter. Set aside. Sauté chopped mushrooms and onions in butter until almost dry. Add flour, seasonings, and half-and-half and cook until thickened. Let mixture cool. Then spread half of the bread rounds with mixture and top with other half of rounds. Brush each round with melted butter and keep in the refrigerator until ready to use, or if not used within 2 days, freeze. When ready to use, fry in an electric skillet at 275° in equal parts of vegetable oil and butter (start with about 2 tablespoons of each) until hot and toasty. Serve immediately.

We had called these fried mushroom sandwiches until one night some little boys were at the Hall attending their grandparents' fiftieth wedding anniversary party. The servers came into the kitchen and said the little boys were in the parlor asking for some more Little Macs. I knew exactly what they wanted and the name has stuck ever since.

AVOCADO MOUSSE WITH CREAMY SHRIMP DRESSING

SERVES 10 TO 12

SALAD

3 envelopes unflavored gelatin
¾ cup cold water
1 cup boiling water
5 ripe avocados, peeled (enough to make about 4 cups)
5 tablespoons lemon juice

2½ tablespoons onion, finely grated
1¾ teaspoon salt
¾ teaspoon sugar
⅓ teaspoon cayenne pepper
¾ cup Hellmann's mayonnaise

In small mixing bowl, dissolve gelatin in cold water, then add boiling water and stir until completely dissolved. Chill until like thin syrup, being careful not to let it get too thick. In the meantime, mash avocados to a purée and add the lemon juice immediately to keep it from darkening. Mix in gelatin.

Add onion and seasonings. Fold in mayonnaise. Pour into a 9″ x 11″ flat glass casserole. Refrigerate for at least 4 hours. When ready to serve, cut into squares and put on green leaf lettuce and cover with dressing.

DRESSING

2 cups sour cream
½ cup ketchup
1½ tablespoons prepared horseradish
2½ tablespoons Worcestershire sauce
1½ tablespoons onion, grated
2 tablespoons lemon juice

1 teaspoon salt
1 teaspoon paprika
¼ teaspoon dry mustard
1 small clove garlic, pressed
1¼ pounds shrimp, cooked, peeled, and cut up

Mix together all ingredients, folding in shrimp last. I prefer to make this dressing the day before it is to be used so the flavors can blend.

When boiling shrimp be careful not to overcook. Boil water with some lemon juice and garlic salt. Add shrimp and when it turns pink, it's done. Immediately pour ice over the drained shrimp to keep it from cooking further. This is not truly a mousse, but it is very light.

BEEF TENDERLOIN WITH SAUTEED MUSHROOMS AND BÉARNAISE SAUCE

SERVES 8

1 whole beef tenderloin, weighing 5 to 6
  pounds
salt

lemon pepper
Lea & Perrins Worcestershire sauce
Lea & Perrins steak sauce

Have your butcher trim all the fat and sinew from the tenderloin. Three hours before cooking time, sprinkle both sides with salt and lemon pepper. Then pour Worcestershire and steak sauces liberally over both sides. Let sit in cooking pan in marinade until time to cook. Cook at 425° for 35 minutes for rare, 40 minutes for medium, and 45 minutes for well done, depending on size of tenderloin. Remove from oven and let sit for 5 minutes. Slice, allowing 2 slices per person. This should feed 8. If using as a heavy hors d'oeuvre on a buffet, slice thin and serve with small rolls and spreads. Allow one tenderloin for 20 people, if using in this manner.

SAUTÉED MUSHROOMS

1 pound mushrooms, washed and sliced
4 green onions, cleaned and sliced thinly
4 tablespoons butter

salt and pepper to taste
dash of garlic and parsley salt
3 teaspoons Worcestershire sauce

After preparing mushrooms and green onions, sauté them in a skillet with the butter. Stir in seasonings and cook for about 5 minutes.

BÉARNAISE SAUCE

½ cup tarragon vinegar
slice of onion
½ teaspoon dried tarragon
½ pound butter

6 egg yolks, beaten
dash of cayenne pepper
1 teaspoon chives, chopped

Boil vinegar with slice of onion and dried tarragon until reduced by half. Meanwhile, melt butter and let stand. In top of double boiler, over hot water (never boiling) combine the vinegar and the egg yolks. Beat in melted butter with a wire whisk, being careful not to use the milky water that accumulates under the melted butter. Beat constantly until thick. Remove from heat and add cayenne pepper and chopped chives.

Spoon sauce onto plates. Place meat slices on top of sauce, and mushrooms on top of meat.

This is our most popular entrée for rehearsal dinners. When it is not served, we are asked, "Where's the beef?"

WILD RICE WITH ALMONDS

SERVES 8

2 boxes Uncle Ben's long grain and wild
  rice (original recipe with herbs and
  spices)
½ cup butter

4 cups chicken broth
1 cup dry white wine
1 cup sliced almonds, toasted slightly
¼ cup parsley, chopped

Melt butter in pan and sauté the rice over medium heat, being careful not to brown. Add seasoning packets, chicken broth, and wine. Bring to a boil and transfer to a deep glass casserole, cover with foil, and bake at 350° for 1 hour. Stir in almonds and parsley.

If you are not serving mushrooms with the beef, add a 6-ounce jar of them to the rice when you add the broth.

Ask anyone around here. Rice is a staple at our house; sometimes we serve it twice a day. There are so many wonderful ways to fix it, and it's a great source of energy.

FRESH ASPARAGUS

SERVES 8

3 pounds asparagus
salt

melted butter
pimiento for garnish

When preparing asparagus, we cut off the tough ends and try to keep the stalks all the same length for a prettier presentation. Wash the asparagus thoroughly to remove all grit. If the stalks are large it will be necessary to peel them from about halfway down the stem to the bottom. Fill a large flat pan with water and bring to a boil. Add salt. Then lay asparagus flat into the boiling water. Boil until the asparagus turns a bright green and is barely tender, about 2 to 3 minutes, depending on size. Use tongs to bring the asparagus out of the water and drain on cookie sheets lined with paper towels.

Serve immediately with melted butter poured over and garnished with pimiento.

If using on a cocktail buffet, upon taking asparagus out of the water, immediately plunge into ice water to stop the cooking process. Then proceed to drain on towels and refrigerate until serving time. Serve with light curry sauce found on page 106.

There is nothing more elegant and delicious to serve anytime than fresh asparagus. Please learn to "undercook" it.

HOME-MAID ROLLS

SERVES 25

4 cups 2 percent milk
1 cup Crisco
1 cup sugar
3 packages dry yeast
7 tablespoons lukewarm water

6½ to 7 cups all-purpose flour
¾ tablespoon salt
1 teaspoon baking soda
1 teaspoon baking powder
½ cup all-purpose flour

Heat Crisco, milk, and sugar until lukewarm and sugar is melted. Sprinkle yeast over water in large bowl and stir until well mixed. Add a little warm milk to yeast mixture to thin and then start adding flour and milk alternately until well mixed, ending with a flour addition. You will know when you have enough flour—dough will be soft. Cover dough with a towel and place in a warm, draft-free place and let rise until it doubles in size, about 1½ hours. Punch down dough and add the salt, baking soda, and baking powder, along with the additional ½ cup flour. Gently stir in. Cover dough again and refrigerate until ready to use.

Dough will keep in refrigerator for about one week. When ready to use, take out the portion you need and knead one or two minutes on floured board. Roll out and cut with round cutter. Brush with melted butter and fold over for pocketbook rolls. Place on a buttered baking sheet and allow to rise again for about 1½ hours. Bake at 425° until brown. Letting the dough rise before refrigeration helps the dough retain its rising power. The dough will rise some in the refrigerator but can be punched down.

We call these "home-maid" because having them made up in the refrigerator is just like having a maid to help you at the last minute.

COLD LEMON MOUSSE CAKE WITH HOT RASPBERRY SAUCE

SERVES 20

CAKE

3 envelopes unflavored gelatin
½ cup cold water
7 large egg yolks, beaten
1 cup lemon juice, freshly squeezed
½ teaspoon salt
2 cups sugar
2½ teaspoons lemon peel, grated

½ teaspoon lemon extract
7 large egg whites, stiffly beaten
2 cups whipping cream, whipped
2 dozen ladyfingers, split
20 maraschino cherries
⅔ cup sliced almonds, toasted

Line 2 9″ x 5″ loaf pans with plastic wrap, letting the wrap extend over the pan at least an inch. Set aside.

Sprinkle gelatin over water in a cup. Set aside. Mix together the egg yolks, lemon juice, salt, and 1 cup of the sugar in top of a double boiler. Cook over slightly boiling water until thickened. Remove from heat and stir in lemon peel, extract, and gelatin. Cool until it just begins to gel. Beat egg whites to soft peaks stage and gradually add the other cup of sugar, beating until stiff. Fold egg whites into lemon mixture. Whip the cream and fold 1 cup of the cream into the mixture.

Make one layer of split ladyfingers along the bottom of the loaf pans lengthwise. Pour in half of the mousse. Make another layer of split ladyfingers on top of the mousse. Pour in the rest of the mousse. You may have mousse remaining, which you can put in custard cups or a bowl. Refrigerate mousse cake until serving time. Lift out the cakes and put on a silver or beautiful glass tray. It is easy to lift out by pulling on the extended plastic wrap. "Frost" cakes with the remaining whipped cream. Make a row of cherries down the length of the cakes. Sprinkle with toasted almonds. Slice to serve, as you would bread, pouring a little raspberry sauce crosswise over each slice.

SAUCE

1 10-ounce package frozen raspberries, thawed

Put thawed raspberries and juice in blender and whirl. Then strain through a fine sieve to remove seeds. Add sugar and Amaretto, stir and refrigerate. Heat before serving.

2 tablespoons superfine sugar
1 tablespoon Amaretto

Take that gorgeous dessert right into the dining room and serve it to your guests. What could make it more "special"? Your guests will appreciate your artistry and you will appreciate the fanfare.

DAUBE GLACÉ

SERVES 20

2 pounds of very lean, thick beef round or
  rump
2 bay leaves
2 large onions, sliced
2 green onions
½ teaspoon thyme
2 sprigs parsley
4 ribs celery
6 whole cloves

1 teaspoon crushed red pepper
1 tablespoon salt
2 quarts water
2 envelopes plain gelatin
½ cup cold water
2 tablespoons lemon juice
2 tablespoons parsley, finely chopped
salt to taste, black pepper to taste

Place the beef and the next 9 ingredients in a large pot with 2 quarts of water and simmer until the beef is tender, skimming the foam off the top as it rises during the first half hour. When the beef is tender the liquid should be reduced to about 1 quart. Take the meat out of the pot and remove any fat or gristle. Finely shred the meat. Strain the liquid. I use one layer of cheesecloth in a strainer. Soak the 2 envelopes of gelatin in ½ cup of cold water, then pour in the quart of hot liquid from the pot and stir. Cool the liquid and add the lemon juice, parsley, and now the shredded meat. Now, season with salt and lots of ground pepper. When it cools, the pepper flavor seems to disappear, so don't be too afraid. Chill this in a ring mold, muffin tins, or anything you choose, according to your needs. In cupcake molds or custard cups it makes a wonderful summer salad topped with homemade mayonnaise. In small muffin tins you can use a Ritz cracker underneath each mold for a wonderful hors d'oeuvre, as intended in this menu. Top off with a little homemade mayonnaise.

SHRIMP REMOULADE

SERVES 8

3 pounds medium shrimp, cooked and
  cleaned
1 heaping tablespoon of garlic, chopped
  fine
1 tablespoon paprika
1 cup Zatarins mustard (creole mustard)
½ cup Wesson oil
¼ cup white wine vinegar

2 tablespoons celery, chopped
2 tablespoons celery tops, chopped
2 tablespoons green onion tops, chopped
2 tablespoons parsley, chopped
salt and pepper to taste
dash Worcestershire sauce
¼ cup sherry

Mix garlic, paprika, mustard, and blend well. Add alternately the oil and the vinegar. Stir in the chopped vegetables and the seasonings, adding the sherry last. You may add more sherry if you like. Marinate the shrimp in this sauce at least 2 hours; overnight will make it even better. It will keep several days in the refrigerator and even freezes well. Serve it on a bed of shredded lettuce.

This recipe was given to me by a mentor, Laura Young. She had the reputation of being the "best cook in Meridian." Being good friends, I was the lucky recipient of many of her most prized recipes, and she had a story for each one of them. This story is so secret that I dare not share where this recipe came from.

ARTICHOKE CHICKEN

SERVES 18

1½ cups butter
10 ounces fresh mushrooms, washed and
  sliced
8 cups white meat of chicken, cooked and
  cubed
4 cans artichoke hearts, quartered
15 tablespoons flour

3 cups whole milk
2 cups whipping cream
1 cup dry sherry
2 teaspoons salt
1 tablespoon Worcestershire sauce
¾ teaspoon white pepper
2 cups Parmesan cheese, freshly grated

Melt ¼ cup butter and sauté mushrooms in the butter. Melt remaining butter in large saucepan and blend in flour and let cook for 1 minute. Slowly add milk and stir and cook to make a white sauce. Stir in cream, add sherry, salt, pepper, and Worcestershire. Place chicken, mushrooms, and artichokes in casserole. Cover with sauce. Top with cheese. Refrigerate overnight. Before serving, bake at 350° for 30 to 40 minutes until hot, brown, and bubbly. You may need to divide this into more than one casserole, depending on the size of your dish. Serve over hot rice.

Linda Townes of Grenada, Mississippi, sent me this recipe after she served it at a beautiful cocktail buffet she gave for our daughter and her then husband-to-be (and Linda's nephew), Andrew Townes. The party was a tremendous success due in part to this divine dish (which she had to make four times) and a twenty-five-pound chocolate cake she had flown in from Dallas. It was a dome-shaped chocolate cake with a chocolate pecan filling between the layers, iced with white chocolate, overlaid with dark chocolate and huge Godiva chocolate curls on top and all around it. When you are in the food business, there are some food items you never forget, and that cake was definitely one of them. I felt I had looked sin in the eye—and happily succumbed.

CARROTS AND PISTACHIOS AND COINTREAU

SERVES 6

1 pound carrots, sliced very thin
3 tablespoons water
3 tablespoons butter

1½ teaspoons salt
½ cup pistachios, chopped
3 tablespoons Cointreau

Place thinly sliced carrots in ice water in refrigerator overnight, until they curl slightly. In a heavy saucepan, combine carrots with water and butter and salt. Bring to a quick boil and reduce to moderately low heat. Cover and cook for 5 minutes. Uncover, and cook for another 3 minutes, or until just tender: the time will vary with the thickness of the carrots. Stir. Transfer to a heated serving dish and add ½ cup of chopped pistachios and Cointreau to taste.

You will need to double or triple this to go with the amount of artichoke-chicken in this menu.

FRENCH CHOCOLATE MOUSSE

SERVES 6 TO 8

6 ounces of semisweet chocolate morsels
4 eggs, separated
1 tablespoon rum

½ pint whipping cream, whipped
2 ounces sliced almonds, toasted

Melt the chocolate over very low heat. Set aside, but keep warm. Beat the egg yolks until pale and lemon-colored. Stir the warm chocolate into the egg yolks and blend well. Beat the egg whites until stiff but not dry. Add a third of the whites to the chocolate and yolk mixture, and then add the rum. Mix well. Carefully fold in the remaining whites. Spoon into pots de crème cups. Chill, covered, at least 8 hours before serving. Top with whipped cream and toasted almonds.

This is lighter than most mousses because it has no cream. If you serve it in small portions, like the pots de crème or custard cups, you can leave the table feeling guiltless.

Sliced Beef Tenderloin/"Home-Maid" rolls/spreads (see pages 87 and 91)

◆

Little Macs (see page 85)

◆

Cheese Straws

◆

Crab Dip Supreme and Toasted Pita Bread Triangles

◆

Fresh Shrimp Mold

◆

Three-Tier Cheese Pâté

◆

Fresh Asparagus (see page 90)

◆

Curry Dip for Vegetables

◆

Fresh Fruit (see page 80)

◆

Fondue Chocolate for Fruits

◆

Cheesecake Squares (see page 20)

◆

Glazed Pecans

An
Affair
To
Remember

❖

Whether it be a cocktail party or a wedding reception, there are just some occasions that are never forgotten, because the food was so beautifully presented, went together so well, and all tasted so divine.

CHEESE STRAWS

SERVES 15

1 10-ounce stick of Kraft Cracker Barrel
   New York aged reserve cheese, grated
10 tablespoons margarine, softened
½ teaspoon salt

½ teaspoon cayenne
1½ cups all-purpose flour (may need 2
   tablespoons more)

Cream together cheese, margarine, and seasonings. Add flour until of the consistency to go through cookie press. Push through press and bake at 325° for about 12 minutes.

A most versatile item to have packed away in tins. They even freeze well. Great for brunches, wine and cheese parties, and as take-alongs for football games.

CRAB DIP SUPREME AND TOASTED PITA BREAD TRIANGLES

SERVES 40

4 8-ounce packages cream cheese
½ cup butter, melted
3 tablespoons lemon juice
3 teaspoons Tabasco
2 tablespoons Worcestershire sauce
5 tablespoons horseradish

1 teaspoon salt
white and cayenne pepper to taste
½ cup chopped green onion tops
2 pounds fresh crabmeat, picked, to
   remove all bones
5 packages white pita bread rounds

Beat cream cheese at medium speed with electric mixer until light and fluffy. Gradually beat in the melted butter. Add all other seasonings but not crabmeat, and mix until well blended. Fold in crabmeat by hand. Taste for seasonings, as you may like it hotter. Place in glass casserole that fits chafing dish and bake at 350° until hot and bubbly and slightly beginning to brown. Keep hot in chafing dish. Serve with toasted pita bread.

Cut each pita bread round into eight triangles, then pull into 2 pieces at the seam. Toast in a 300° oven until light brown.

The pita bread can be done a couple days prior to use, as can the crabmeat dip. We put the pita bread into brown-paper grocery sacks and clip them shut. Refrigerate the crabmeat dip in a very cold place in the refrigerator, until time to cook.

FRESH SHRIMP MOLD

SERVES 100

¼ cup water
juice of 2 lemons
2 envelopes plain gelatin
2 8-ounce packages cream cheese
2 cups sour cream
1 cup mayonnaise
½ cup green onions, chopped
½ cup celery, chopped
½ cup green pepper, chopped

¼ cup pimiento, chopped
½ cup chili sauce
1 tablespoon Worcestershire sauce
1 teaspoon salt
4 pounds shrimp, cooked, shelled, deveined, and cut into 3 or 4 pieces, depending on size of shrimp. You will need 6 cups.

Sprinkle gelatin on top of water and lemon juice in a small custard cup and stir. Place cup in a small saucepan with some water in the bottom and let water simmer for about 8 minutes or until gelatin is dissolved. Remove custard cup and let gelatin cool. Place the cream cheese, sour cream, and mayonnaise in bowl of food processor and thoroughly blend until all lumps of cream cheese are gone. Put cream cheese mixture in a large bowl. Fold in the green onions, celery, green pepper, and pimiento. Add chili sauce, Worcestershire,

and salt. Stir. Fold in shrimp. Fold in gelatin mixture. Pour into a fish mold or appropriate molds and refrigerate until set. Unmold on beautiful tray and decorate. Serve with Ritz crackers. Makes enough for 100 servings on a cocktail buffet.

I always use a fish mold and give the fish eyes of green olives with pimiento, parsley eyelashes, and a mouth of a large piece of pimiento cut as lips. You can give it scales of thin cucumber slices.

THREE-TIER CHEESE PÂTÉ

SERVES 40

6 8-ounce packages cream cheese, softened
1 2-ounce package ranch-style dressing mix
2 cups sharp cheddar cheese, grated
1 4-ounce package blue cheese, crumbled

green onions, chopped
green olives, chopped
crisp bacon, crumbled
black olives, chopped

Spray an 8- or 9-inch cheesecake pan with Pam. In food processor, place 2 packages cream cheese with the dry ranch dressing mix and process. Spread in bottom of cheesecake pan. Place 2 more packages of cream cheese in processor with the 2 cups of grated cheese. Process. Put this layer on top of first layer in cheesecake pan. Put last 2 packages of cream cheese in processor. Add the blue cheese and process. Put this layer on top of last layer in pan. Refrigerate until serving time. Serve on a glass cake stand with crackers. Top it off with pie-shaped triangles of chopped green onions, green olives, crisp crumbled bacon, black olives, etc.

Cheese is always welcome at so many occasions, and this is a good way to serve variety in a pretty manner.

CURRY DIP FOR VEGETABLES

SERVES 8

1 cup Hellmann's mayonnaise
2 teaspoons tarragon vinegar
½ teaspoon salt
dash pepper
⅛ teaspoon thyme

¼ teaspoon curry powder
2 teaspoons chili sauce
2 tablespoons chives, snipped
2 tablespoons onion, grated

Mix all together and refrigerate.

The secret is out! Everyone wants this recipe. This is it. Go ahead and double it because you will use it. My friend Georgane Love, from Hattiesburg, shared this with me many years ago and I have made it so much I could make it in my sleep. When we first opened Hamilton Hall, I did without sleep many nights to cook and did indeed cook in my sleep when I got a chance to lie down.

FONDUE CHOCOLATE FOR FRUITS

MAKES 1½ CUPS

2 tablespoons light corn syrup
⅓ cup half-and-half cream
9 ounces of bar chocolate

2 tablespoons Kirsch, Grand Marnier, or
orange-flavored liqueur

Heat corn syrup and cream together in top of double boiler over hot, but not boiling, water. Add chocolate which has been broken into pieces and stir until chocolate is melted and mixture is smooth. Remove from heat and stir in liqueur. At serving table, keep warm in chafing dish, surrounded by trays of beautiful fruits on long toothpicks.

This is always a hit at any event, so I am sure you will need to double or triple it depending on number of guests. If there is any left, it will keep nicely in refrigerator and can be reheated.

GLAZED PECANS

MAKES 1½ CUPS

½ cup water
½ cup sugar
2 dried red chili peppers

1 cup pecans
¼ cup molasses

Combine water, sugar, and chili peppers in a small saucepan. Over high heat bring to a boil. Add pecans and return to a boil. Lower heat and simmer 10 minutes. Drain nuts from mixture and place nuts on a baking sheet and bake 45 minutes at 250°. Remove pecans from oven, cool; place in a bowl. Add molasses and toss to coat. Return pecans to a greased baking sheet and bake an additional 45 minutes or until pecans are crisp.

A little time-consuming, but you won't be sorry. The chili peppers give them a little bit different flavor, to say the least. Pecans are a big product in Mississippi and the Deep South, and we love to come up with something new for them. This recipe comes to me from my friends Jim and Mary Hefter, who are both wonderful cooks.

Ladies' Luncheon

Cranberry Salad with Orange Salad Dressing

Turkey Divan

Zucchini Bread

English Trifle

◆

Lunch for the Gentlemen

Spinach Salad (see page 31)

Seafood Stuffed Eggplant

Quick Rolls (see page 42)

Nut-Crusted Ice Cream Balls with Praline Sauce

◆

Formal Dinner Party

Sublime Seafood Salad

Individual Beef Wellingtons with Brown Sauce

Spinach Artichoke Casserole

Broiled Tomatoes Oregano

Cherries Jubilee

A
Christmas
Affair

❖

Christmas is the ideal time for entertaining, and it is "the season" here at Hamilton Hall. Whether it be a luncheon for the ladies, a party for the gentlemen, or a formal dinner party, everyone is in the mood for a festive occasion.

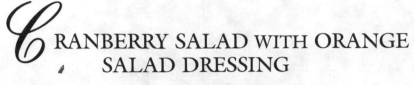

CRANBERRY SALAD WITH ORANGE SALAD DRESSING

MAKES 14 INDIVIDUAL MOLDS

SALAD

1 6-ounce package raspberry Jell-O
2¾ cups boiling water
1 8-ounce package cream cheese
1 15-ounce can crushed pineapple, drained

1 16-ounce can cranberries, whole or
    jellied
1 cup pecans, chopped

Dissolve Jell-O in boiling water. Set aside to cool. Whip cream cheese with a small amount of the pineapple juice to soften. When well mixed, fold in the pineapple, cranberries, and nuts. When the gelatin starts to congeal, fold in the mixture. Chill until firm. Serve on individual lettuce-leaf cups with the following dressing:

DRESSING

1 4½-ounce carton frozen whipped
    topping

¼ cup Hellmann's mayonnaise
¼ cup instant Tang

Mix ingredients together and refrigerate.

I find the cream cheese, pineapple, and cranberries blend best by using the food processor. Just be careful and don't overprocess and do not put the nuts in the food processor. Fold them in last. You will use this recipe time and time again as we do, because it is so well received by family and guests alike.

TURKEY DIVAN

SERVES 6

1 5-pound turkey breast, baked and sliced
2 bunches of fresh broccoli, cleaned, large
    stalks trimmed off, and cooked only
    until it turns bright green
1 cup Hellmann's mayonnaise
2 10¾-ounce cans cream of chicken soup
2 teaspoons lemon juice

1 teaspoon Worcestershire sauce
½ teaspoon dry mustard
½ teaspoon curry powder
¾ cup New York sharp cheddar cheese,
    shredded
6 slices white bread, crumbled
2 tablespoons butter, cut in small bits

Using a 9″ x 13″ flat glass casserole, place a layer of turkey and then a layer of broccoli. Mix together the mayonnaise, soup, lemon juice, Worcestershire sauce, dry mustard, and curry powder. Then stir in grated cheese. Pour this over the broccoli. Top with bread and little pieces of butter. Bake at 350° for about 30 minutes or until bubbly and the bread cubes are toasty. This feeds 6, depending on how large a serving you make. Lift out each serving with a spatula to place it on the serving plates. You will probably have enough broccoli and turkey slices for 2 casseroles, but you will have to double the sauce recipe.

This is the very first dish I served at Hamilton Hall at the first luncheon. When purchasing the house, I told the real estate agent what I had in mind doing, but I really didn't know how to get started and whether anyone would come there. She said her garden club was to have a luncheon in November and she was hostess so she would have the first party at Hamilton Hall. Sinch we moved in on September 17, I had to hurry to get everything ready. Thank goodness, it was a big success. We were booked every day from December 1 through December 19.

ZUCCHINI BREAD

SERVES 20

3 cups flour
1½ cups sugar
1 teaspoon salt
4½ teaspoons baking powder
1 cup pecans or walnuts, chopped

4 eggs, beaten
⅔ cup salad oil
2 cups zucchini, washed, dried, grated,
    but not peeled
3 teaspoons lemon rind, grated

Stir together the flour, sugar, salt, baking powder, and nuts in a large mixing bowl. Mix together the eggs, oil, zucchini, and rind. Add to flour mixture. Bake at 350° for about 1 hour in 2 greased 9″ x 5″ loaf pans. Cool before slicing.

The lemon rind is what gives this bread such an exceptional flavor. The bread is especially pretty to use at Christmas because of the green peel of the zucchini.

ENGLISH TRIFLE

SERVES 10

24 ladyfingers or thin slices of pound cake
1 cup black raspberry jam
2 cups sliced fresh frozen peaches
3 bananas, sliced
2 cups fresh strawberries, sliced

½ cup sherry
1 recipe boiled custard (see page 127)
1 10-ounce package frozen raspberries
1 cup whipping cream, whipped
½ cup sliced almonds, toasted

Split the ladyfingers and cover one side with the jam and replace tops. Line a trifle or big glass bowl with the ladyfingers. Sprinkle with the sherry. Add, in layers, the peaches, bananas, and strawberries. Pour cold custard over the fruit. Put the raspberries on top. Cover with the whipped cream and then the toasted almonds.

Be sure to bring the beautiful bowl to the buffet and serve in the dining room, as it makes such a nice presentation. Serve in stemmed sherbets, reaching down all the way in the serving bowl to make sure that each serving has some of everything.

SEAFOOD STUFFED EGGPLANT

SERVES 8

4 medium to large eggplants, washed, stems removed, and cut in half

1 cup onions, chopped

1 cup green onions, chopped

5 cloves garlic, finely chopped

1 cup green peppers, chopped

½ cup celery, chopped

2 bay leaves

1 teaspoon thyme

3½ teaspoons salt

½ teaspoon black pepper

4 tablespoons bacon drippings

1½ pounds medium shrimp, shells and veins removed, uncooked

1 pound fresh crabmeat, picked over for bones

¼ pound butter

½ teaspoon Tabasco

1 tablespoon Worcestershire sauce

5 slices white bread, crumbled

2 eggs, beaten

¼ cup fresh parsley, chopped

12 tablespoons Romano cheese, grated

Cook eggplant halves in boiling salted water until tender, being careful to keep shell intact. Let cool a little, and scoop out the eggplant with a large spoon (a small ice scoop with sharp edges works wonderfully well). Chop the eggplant. Place the shells in a long shallow baking dish. In a large heavy saucepan sauté the onions, green onions, garlic, green pepper, celery, and bay leaves in bacon drippings for 20 minutes. Add thyme, salt, and pepper. Add chopped eggplant and cover. Cook, stirring occasionally with a wooden spoon, for 30 minutes. In a separate skillet, sauté the shrimp in the butter until they turn pink, about 2 or 3 minutes, depending on the size of the shrimp, but being careful not to overcook. Add the shrimp to the eggplant. Mix the Tabasco, Worcestershire sauce, bread, and eggs together and add this to the eggplant. Stir in the parsley and lemon juice and mix well. Gently fold in the crabmeat. Remove the bay leaves. Stuff eggplant shells with the eggplant mixture and sprinkle with 1½ tablespoons Romano cheese and bake at 350° for about 40 minutes.

Fabulous! Everyone will want to stay for dinner to see what else you have.

$\mathscr{N}$UT-CRUSTED ICE CREAM BALLS WITH PRALINE SAUCE

SERVES 10 TO 12

ICE CREAM BALLS

½ gallon vanilla ice cream

1 pound pecans, chopped

Chop pecans to a medium size. The amount you need will depend on how heavily you apply them to the ice cream balls.

Slightly soften vanilla ice cream. Mold into large balls. Roll ice cream balls into pecans. Return to freezer to harden.

SAUCE

1½ cups dark brown sugar
¼ cup butter

⅔ cup white corn syrup
⅔ cup evaporated milk

Combine in a medium saucepan the sugar, butter, and corn syrup. Let mixture come to a boil, stirring constantly over a medium low heat. Insert candy thermometer into mixture and let mixture cook to 240°. Remove from heat and let it cool a little bit. Add ⅔ cup evaporated milk. Stir thoroughly. You may refrigerate until ready to use and reheat, or keep warm on stove until serving time. Place ice cream balls

on individual serving plates. Pour sauce over each ball and top with a dollop of whipped cream and a maraschino cherry with a stem.

This is a wonderful make-ahead dessert that you can keep made up all the time. The problem is that if anyone knows they are in the freezer and the sauce is in the refrigerator, they will be gone before you know it!

SUBLIME SEAFOOD SALAD

SERVES 8

1 pound shrimp, boiled, shelled, and
deveined
1 pound fresh crabmeat, picked over to
remove bones
4 fresh tomatoes, chopped
4 green onions, finely chopped, white and
green parts
1 cup Hellmann's mayonnaise
2 tablespoons horseradish

1 tablespoon Worcestershire sauce
¼ cup fresh parsley, chopped
juice of 1 lemon
salt and white pepper to taste
2 tablespoons capers, well drained
8 large pieces green curly-leaf lettuce
1 head iceberg lettuce, shredded
paprika
black olives

Combine the mayonnaise, horseradish, and lemon juice. Add the tomatoes, green onions, and parsley. Add salt and pepper and taste for seasonings, remembering that the capers are salty. Gently fold in the capers. Refrigerate until serving time. On each salad plate place a piece of curly green lettuce. Then make a bed of shredded lettuce. Evenly divide the shrimp and crabmeat among the

plates and top with the dressing. Sprinkle with paprika and large black olives.

Every Christmas dinner my children call for this to be on the menu. Our son, Steve, is especially fond of seafood. The first time I served this, he looked up and said "outstanding," and I knew I had a winner.

INDIVIDUAL BEEF WELLINGTONS WITH BROWN SAUCE

SERVES 8

BEEF WELLINGTONS

8 5-ounce beef fillets
olive oil
salt and pepper to taste
1½ pounds fresh mushrooms, finely
    chopped

1 tablespoon butter
2 tablespoons shallots, finely chopped
¼ cup dry Madeira wine
8 frozen patty shells, thawed but unbaked
1 egg, lightly beaten

Freeze fillets for 20 minutes. Remove from freezer and brush with oil and salt and pepper. Brown in a hot skillet for a very few minutes on each side, around 5 minutes, but it will depend on whether they are small and thick or big and not as thick. Place on cookie sheet and refrigerate. Put the chopped mushrooms, a small amount at a time, in the corner of a tea towel and squeeze out as much water as possible. Plan for this to take a few minutes. When all are done, sauté the mushrooms for 7 to 8 minutes in the butter with the shallots. When the mushrooms are breaking up, add the Madeira and boil rapidly until liquid is evaporated. Season with a small amount of salt and pepper. Refrigerate until ready to put the Wellingtons together.

Roll each patty shell out to a rectangle about ⅛ inch thick. Doing one at a time, place an eighth of the mushroom mixture in the middle of the pastry and top with one fillet. Fold over one side; then one end piece, the other side, and finally the other end. Seal with damp fingers. Place seam side down on a cookie sheet. Brush with beaten egg and bake at 450°: 10 minutes for rare, 12 minutes for medium-rare, and 15 minutes for medium. Top with brown sauce and a piece of parsley. I serve the sauce on the side.

SAUCE

¼ cup onion, minced
½ teaspoon sugar
2 tablespoons butter
2 tablespoons flour
2 cups beef consommé

⅛ teaspoon pepper
¼ teaspoon thyme
1 bay leaf
2 teaspoons tomato paste

Sauté the onion and sugar in the butter for 5 minutes. Gradually stir in the flour and cook over low heat. Stir constantly until brown. Gradually pour in the consommé. You must stir this mixture until it reaches a boil. Then add the pepper, thyme, bay leaf, and tomato paste and cook over low heat for about 20 minutes. Strain. This may be made ahead and refrigerated.

Sometimes I make cutouts from the leftover pastry to decorate the top of the Wellingtons. The egg will keep them in place. This is the easiest brown sauce you will ever make.

SPINACH ARTICHOKE CASSEROLE

SERVES 8

2 packages frozen chopped spinach
1 can artichoke hearts
1 8-ounce package cream cheese
½ cup butter

1 can sliced water chestnuts
salt and pepper to taste
Italian bread crumbs
Parmesan cheese

Cook spinach according to directions and drain well, pushing a wooden spoon against the colander to remove as much water as possible. Drain the artichokes and slice. Place artichokes in bottom of buttered casserole. Melt the cream cheese in a medium saucepan with the butter. Add the spinach and water chestnuts and mix well. Salt and pepper to taste. Pour over the artichokes. Top with Italian bread crumbs and Parmesan cheese. Bake 30 minutes at 350°.

Two wonderful vegetables put together so easily in a wonderful casserole that can be made ahead. What more could you ask for?

BROILED TOMATOES OREGANO

SERVES 8

4 large tomatoes, halved, or 8 small
   tomatoes, tops cut off
olive oil
salt and pepper to taste

tiny bit sugar
1 teaspooon oregano
½ cup grated Parmesan cheese
buttered bread crumbs

Place tomatoes in a long, flat glass baking dish. Brush lightly with a little olive oil. Sprinkle with salt and pepper and a tiny bit of sugar. Broil 5 minutes, 4 inches from heat. Mix oregano with bread crumbs and sprinkle evenly over the tomatoes. Top with cheese and broil until lightly browned.

A group of Japanese educators was in our city to attend a seminar at our local university, and we were to entertain them for dinner. Much thought was given to the menu—we wanted them to experience the Deep South. We knew we were going to start with mint juleps on the porch, but we debated for days between poultry and beef. Finally, the decision was made to serve Cornish hens.

The first part of the evening went very well, but during the main course the servers came to the kitchen and said our guests of honor were not eating the Cornish hens. We were quite concerned, so when I saw the host in the hallway, I asked him if everything was all right. He replied that it was all delicious— especially the hens. Later, we noticed that the local educators had cleaned their plates, but to my dismay I learned that the Japanese gentlemen were not only educators, they were also of an order of Buddhist Monks who were disinclined to eat "anything that breaks the air." Bad choice, don't you think? You will note that there is no recipe in this book for Cornish hens.

CHERRIES JUBILEE

SERVES 8

½ gallon vanilla ice cream, slightly
   softened
1 16-ounce can dark sweet cherries
1 tablespoon cornstarch
¼ cup sugar

1 tablespoon butter
2 tablespoons kirsch
2 tablespoons brandy
2 tablespoons 150-proof rum

Scoop ice cream into individual serving dishes that can go into the freezer. Place dishes in freezer until serving time.

Carefully drain the juice from the cherries. You should have 1 cup of juice. If you don't, add water to make it a cup. Bring juice to a boil in a 2-quart saucepan. Mix cornstarch and sugar. Add a little of the juice to the cornstarch and sugar mixture and stir. Return it to the boiling juice. Boil 1 minute. Add the cherries. Remove from the heat; add the butter, the kirsch, and the brandy. Transfer to a flambé pan. Heat, add the rum, and ignite. Spoon cherries with sauce over the dishes of ice cream.

Nothing will impress your guests more than a flaming dessert served right from the buffet in the dining room. A copper Sterno burner flambé pan is a wonderful investment. We have found that the foolproof liqueur to ignite with is the 150-proof rum. It produces a beautiful blue flame, but stand back. The first time we did it at Hamilton Hall, we used too much rum and the flame was very intense. If we had not had thirteen-foot ceilings, the flame might have reached the top of the room. It made a big impression on our guests and we tried to recover from our scare and act as if we did it like that all the time.

Praline Cheesecake with Praline Sauce

◆

Boiled Custard and Fruitcake Cookies

◆

Flaming Baked Alaska

◆

Bananas Foster

◆

Homemade Ice Cream and Pound Cake

◆

Frozen Amaretto Cream with Raspberry Sauce

◆

Champagne Ice

◆

Mrs. Carleton's Coconut Cake

◆

Orange Date Nut Cake

◆

Pralines

◆

Dessert Coffee Drinks

❖

A
Sweet
Affair

❖

Although you have found dessert recipes throughout the book, the recipes in this section are as sweet as the South. We hope they will tantalize your taste buds and give you a desire to taste our sweetness by making a visit soon.

PRALINE CHEESECAKE WITH PRALINE SAUCE

SEVES 10 TO 12

CRUST

1⅓ cups graham cracker crumbs
4 tablespoons sugar

4 tablespoons butter, melted

FILLING

4 8-ounce packages cream cheese, softened
1⅔ cups dark brown sugar, packed
4 eggs, beaten

2½ tablespoons flour
⅔ cup pecans, finely chopped
2 teaspoons vanilla

TOPPING

1 recipe praline sauce (page 117)
1 cup whipping cream, whipped

¾ cup pecans, chopped and toasted

Combine crumbs, sugar, and butter. Press in bottom of a 10-inch springform pan. Bake in a 350° oven for 10 minutes. Combine cream cheese, sugar, and flour. Mix at medium mixer-speed until well blended and fluffy. Add eggs, one at a time, beating after each addition. Blend in vanilla and pecans. Pour mixture over crumbs and bake at 350° for 55 minutes or until set. Cool before removing from pan. Chill before serving. Pour warm praline sauce over each serving of cheesecake. Top with whipped cream and additional toasted pecans.

Nothing can be finer for dessert.

BOILED CUSTARD

SERVES 6

4 cups sweet milk
6 eggs, lightly beaten
¾ cup sugar

⅛ teaspoon salt
2 teaspoons vanilla

Scald milk in top of double boiler. Beat eggs with sugar and salt. Stir a little of the hot milk into the egg mixture, then stir the egg mixture back into the rest of the milk. Cook and stir in the double boiler, never allowing the water in the bottom of boiler to boil. Stir constantly, moving the pan around a bit, to keep from having hot spots. The mixture will be done when it feels thick when stirred and coats the back of a wooden spoon. Remove from heat. Stir for another minute or two, cover, and let cool. When slightly cool, strain and add vanilla. Refrigerate until very cold.

Silly name for something that you dare not let boil, or even the water boil that you are cooking it over! It takes a little extra time and care to make this, but you will reap a reward. This is a real southern dessert that many southerners prefer over eggnog with their fruitcake. Top with meringues and you have Floating Islands, or use as the custard for English Trifle. Best yet, add a little bourbon to each cupful.

FRUITCAKE COOKIES

MAKES 8 TO 10 DOZEN

1 cup margarine
2 cups light brown sugar
2 eggs, beaten
½ cup buttermilk
3½ cups plain flour

1 teaspoon baking soda
1 teaspoon salt
1½ cups pecans, chopped
2 cups candied cherries, chopped
2 cups chopped dates

Cream margarine and sugar until fluffy. Add eggs and beat well. Stir in buttermilk. Sift together dry ingredients and add to the butter mixture, mixing well. Toss cherries with a little sugar to keep them from sticking together. Add pecans, dates, and cherries to batter. Drop by teaspoons onto greased cookie sheet and bake at 350° for 10 to 12 minutes.

These are great to have at Christmastime. They can easily take the place of fruitcake and are a lot easier, keeping well in airtight tins. What a nice gift to give.

FLAMING BAKED ALASKA

SERVES 10

1 1-pound Sara Lee pound cake
½ gallon Neapolitan brick ice cream
6 egg whites
salt

1 teaspoon lemon juice
1 cup confectioners' sugar
150-proof rum for igniting

Slice the pound cake into 5 horizontal layers. A large bread knife or sharp chef's knife does this very well. Lay the first layer down in the bottom of a stainless-steel platter, or any oven dish. Measure off your block of ice cream to the width of the cake and slice through the block on one side. You will lose part of one side of the chocolate or strawberry. Place the large block of ice cream on top of the layer of pound cake and cut and fill in the back portion of the layer with the remaining portion of ice cream, until you create a pound cake shape. Place a layer of pound cake lengthwise on either side of the ice cream and cut one layer of cake into 2 pieces for the ends. Place the remaining layer on top, completely encasing the ice cream with the cake. Trim and cut pieces as you need to for a neat fit. Should you desire,

purchase 2 blocks of ice cream and then you can cut them both for a neater fit and you can save the remaining portion of ice cream for another meal. Place the encased ice cream in the freezer until ready to use. At time of serving, preheat your oven to 425°. Beat the egg whites with the salt until frothy. Add lemon juice and confectioners' sugar gradually, and continue to beat until the meringue is glossy and thick and stands in peaks. Remove ''cake'' from freezer and completely cover top and sides with a 1-inch layer of meringue. Swirl remaining meringue on top of cake lavishly. Bake in hot oven (425°) for 6 to 8 minutes or until meringue is lightly browned. Remove from oven and pour rum over cake and ignite. Make your presentation quickly and slice and serve.

BANANAS FOSTER

SERVES 4 TO 6

½ gallon french vanilla ice cream

Prior to preparing sauce, put ice cream into individual serving bowls and put back in freezer.

2 large bananas
1 cup brown sugar
1 teaspoon cinnamon

⅓ cup butter
⅓ cup banana liqueur
½ cup kirsch

In heavy skillet or flambé pan, melt butter slowly. Add brown sugar and cinnamon and heat mixture slowly until it bubbles. Cut bananas in thirds and then cut lengthwise. Put bananas, cut side down, into sauce. Cook slowly until bananas are barely tender. Spoon hot sauce over bananas while cooking. Add banana liqueur and heat until it bubbles. Pour kirsch carefully over sauce and ignite. Spoon over bowls of ice cream and serve immediately.

New Orleans restaurants are famous for this, but there is no reason it can't be done tableside right in your own dining room. We put the ice cream in the bowls early in the day and measure out the sauce ingredients in the flambé pan in the afternoon and then forget it until coffee is being served. Spectacular!

HOMEMADE ICE CREAM

SERVES 8

4 eggs, beaten until very light
2 cups sugar
4 cups milk, warmed

2 cups whipping cream
1 teaspoon vanilla extract
½ teaspoon salt

Add sugar to beaten eggs and beat until thick. Add a little of the warm milk to the eggs, stir, and return mixture to the pan of heated milk and cook over low heat until custard coats the back of a spoon. Add whipping cream, salt, and vanilla. Chill at least an hour before freezing in a hand-cranked or electric ice cream freezer. If it's peach season, use the same recipe with 4 cups mashed ripe peaches, omit the vanilla extract, and add almond extract and juice from a half of a lemon.

POUND CAKE

SERVES 8 TO 10

1 cup butter, no substitute
2 cups sugar

6 eggs
2 cups flour

Cream the butter and add the sugar gradually, while beating on a medium speed with your mixer. Cream until it looks a white, light cream color. This will take about 5 to 8 minutes. Then add 3 eggs, one at a time, beating after each addition. Add 1 cup flour and mix. Add the other three eggs, one at a time, beating after each addition. Add the last cup of flour and mix. Beating well in the beginning is the success of this cake, as no baking powder is used, but this should be done before the flour is added. Grease a large tube pan, pour in batter, and bake at 350° for about an hour, or until top of cake is golden and a wonderful crust is formed. You may add 2 teaspoons almond flavoring, if you like, or vanilla or lemon or some of all. But, please, try it plain first. You won't be dissappointed.

Some recipes stand the test of time, and this is surely one of them. It's my mom's favorite cake, and she likes the almond extract. I prefer it plain.

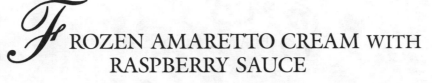

FROZEN AMARETTO CREAM WITH RASPBERRY SAUCE

SERVES 8 TO 10

CREAM

**12 Archway soft macaroon cookies,
   crumbled**
1 tablespoon almond flavoring
½ gallon vanilla ice cream, softened

6 tablespoons Amaretto
2 cups whipping cream, whipped
½ cup sliced almonds, toasted

Put crumbled macaroons in a large bowl and pour almond flavoring over and stir thoroughly. Add softened ice cream, pour on liqueur. Stir all together. Add whipped cream and fold in. Pour into a bundt cake pan; cover and freeze.

SAUCE

3 10-ounce packages frozen raspberries
½ cup sugar

5 tablespoons Amaretto

Simmer berries with sugar until soft. Remove from heat and stir in liqueur. Unmold cream onto cold platter. Sprinkle on the almonds. Pour warm berry sauce over each serving. Should make 12 slices.

You may need to dip the bundt pan into a little warm water to unmold. I always spray the pan with a little Pam and run a knife around the sides before trying to unmold.

This is another dessert that is beautiful for Christmas and can be done ahead.

CHAMPAGNE ICE

SERVES 6 TO 8

¾ cup sugar
1½ cups water
3 tablespoons orange liqueur
1 lemon

2 oranges
3 cups champagne
2 cups strawberries, sliced
extra sugar for the strawberries

Put sugar and water in a saucepan and bring to a boil. Cook 5 minutes. Cool. While this is cooling, squeeze the juice from the oranges and the lemon and reserve the juice. Peel the rind from the lemon and one of the oranges and add the peel to the cooled syrup. Add the orange liqueur. Chill the syrup for 2 hours. Discard the peels. Stir into the syrup mixture 2 cups of champagne and reserved orange and lemon juice. Place this mixture in the freezer until it is mushy and then beat with mixer until smooth. Place back in freezer and stir fairly often, about every 30 minutes, for a fine, snowy texture.

Sprinkle the strawberries with a little sugar and pour the remaining 1 cup of champagne over the strawberries. Let the strawberries stand in the refrigerator at least 4 hours. Serve the strawberries in crystal goblets and top each serving with the champagne ice.

When strawberries are in season we serve them in many different ways. You will find many strawberry recipes in this book for that reason. If it is spring, you can count of their being on the table if you eat at Hamilton Hall.

MRS. CARLETON'S COCONUT CAKE

CAKE

1 cup butter
2 cups sugar
3 cups cake flour, sifted
3 teaspoons baking powder

½ teaspoon salt
1 cup milk
2 teaspoons vanilla
8 egg whites, stiffly beaten

Cream butter and sugar well. Sift the dry ingredients together and add alternately with the milk, beginning and ending with the dry ingredients. Add vanilla. Fold in stiffly beaten egg whites. Bake in 4 9" cake pans, which have been greased and lined with waxed paper. Bake at 325° for 15 minutes or until done. Do not overcook. Remove from oven and cool.

FILLING

3 cups sugar
1½ cups sweet milk

2 fresh coconuts, grated

Cook the sugar with the milk until the mixture thickens enough for the cake to absorb. Spread a little filling on first layer, then put a layer of coconut and then more filling over coconut. Place a second cake layer on top and continue as above until all layers are stacked. Do not put coconut on top layer, just filling. Cover with white icing.

ICING

1½ cups sugar
½ cup water

2 egg whites

Cook sugar and water until mixture comes to hard-boil stage. Beat egg whites. Slowly pour cooked syrup over egg whites while beating to make white icing.

Christmas is just not Christmas in the South without fresh coconut cake. With this recipe you can have a head start, because once the cake is stacked with filling, it can be carefully wrapped and frozen; then you can put the icing on when ready to use.

ORANGE DATE NUT CAKE

1 cup butter
2 cups sugar
4 eggs, well beaten
1⅓ cups buttermilk
4 cups cake flour, with ½ cup kept separate
1 teaspoon baking soda
1 teaspoon salt
1 teaspoon baking powder

1 teaspoon vanilla
2½ tablespoons orange rind, grated
8 to 10 ounces dates, chopped
1½ to 2 cups pecans, chopped
1 cup orange juice
1½ cups sugar
2 tablespoons orange rind, grated

Cream 1 cup butter with the sugar, beating all the while. When light and fluffy add the eggs, beating in by thirds. Add the buttermilk alternately with 3½ cups flour that has been sifted with the baking soda, salt, and baking powder. Sprinkle the other ½ cup flour over the dates, nuts, and orange rind and fold into batter. Add vanilla. Grease a large tube pan on the bottom only and then cut waxed paper to fit the bottom of pan. Do not grease the sides of pan. Bake at 350° for 65 to 70 minutes.

While the cake is baking, cook the orange juice, sugar, and orange rind until thick. When the cake is done, remove from oven, and, leaving cake in pan, punch holes down in cake with an ice pick. Gradually pour orange juice mixture over cake until it is all absorbed into cake. Let stay in pan for 2 days before cutting.

This is my daughter's favorite Christmas cake, and she asks me to bake one each year. It is wonderful because it can be made ahead and stays moist for a very long time.

PRALINES

1 cup sugar, caramelized
3 cups sugar
1 cup milk

4 tablespoons butter
pinch of baking soda
2 cups pecans

To caramelize sugar, place the 1 cup of sugar in a saucepan and cook over medium heat, stirring frequently until it has a wet look. Then stir constantly until a syrup is formed and it is brown and soupy.

Bring the sugar and milk to a boil. Add the caramelized sugar and butter and baking soda. Cook until it forms a soft ball in water, or to soft-ball stage on candy thermometer. Add pecans and beat until creamy. Drop by spoonfuls onto a buttered cookie sheet.

Some inns provide cookies for their guests. Here at Hamilton Hall we provide pralines so they will know they are in the South.

DESSERT COFFEE DRINKS

To make your own hot coffee drinks, start with ½ cup of hot, strong coffee and choose from the suggestions below. Top off your steaming cup with some whipped cream and a large dash of cinnamon or nutmeg.

CAFÉ ALEXANDER: Stir in 1 tablespoon crème de cacao and 1 tablespoon brandy.

CAFÉ BENEDICTINE: Stir in 2 tablespoons Benedictine and 2 tablespoons light cream.

CAFÉ CARIBE: Stir in 1 tablespoon coffee liqueur and 1 tablespoon rum.

CAFÉ COLOMBIAN: Stir in 2 tablespoons coffee liqueur and 1 tablespoon coffee-flavored syrup.

CAFÉ ISRAEL: Stir in 2 tablespoons chocolate-flavored syrup and 2 tablespoons orange liqueur.

CAFÉ NUT: Stir in 2 tablespoons Amaretto or hazelnut liqueur.

DUTCH COFFEE: Stir in 2 tablespoons chocolate-mint liqueur.

IRISH COFFEE: Stir in 1 tablespoon Irish whiskey and 2 teaspoons sugar.

ORANGE-BRANDY COFFEE: Stir in 1 tablespoon orange liqueur and 1 tablespoon brandy. If desired, sprinkle finely shredded orange peel atop whipped cream instead of cinnamon or nutmeg.

$\mathscr{I}$NDEX